THE CLEMENT VISION

Kennikat Press
National University Publications
Literary Criticism Series

General Editor
John E. Becker
Fairleigh Dickinson University

THE CLEMENT VISION

Poetic Realism in Turgenev and James

DALE E. PETERSON

National University Publications
KENNIKAT PRESS • 1975
Port Washington, N.Y. • London

Manufactured in the United States of America

Published by
Kennikat Press Corp.
Port Washington, N.Y. / London

Library of Congress Cataloging in Publication Data

Peterson, Dale L
    The clement vision.

    (Literary criticism series) (National University publications)
    Bibliography: p.
    Includes index.
    1. James, Henry, 1843-1916—Criticism and interpretation. 2. Turgenev, Ivan Sergeevich, 1818-1883—Influence—James. 3. Realism in literature.
PS2124.P4   809'.91'3   75-31614
ISBN 0-8046-9107-X

FOR EARL AND LENA PETERSON

Contents

Acknowledgments

I could never have persisted in this venture had I not been sponsored and sustained by two scholars who assured my freedom of movement between and among the established academic precincts; like James's mentor, Turgenev, they kept "windows open into distances which stretched far beyond the *banlieue*." Certainly I could not have hoped for a more tactful and incisive critic, or a more gentle taskmaster, than Professor Charles Feidelson, Jr. And it would require an elaborate chronicle to list my indebtedness to Professor Victor Erlich; over many years his lively presence has been a constant intellectual stimulus. Others have helped too—more than they themselves realize. I think especially of Robert Louis Jackson and J. Michael Holquist at Yale, and of my colleagues at Amherst College, Leo Marx and John A. Cameron. The critical scrutiny of all these readers has prodded me to think larger thoughts and to ask larger questions as I continue to contemplate the complex relation between literary form and "developing" cultures.

With great fondness, I remember the exceptional kindness of two gracious women, Miss Margaret Perry and Miss Patricia Holsaert. They hosted me on several occasions in Hancock, New Hampshire, and offered me open access to the extant papers and effects in the Perry homestead and archives. I will take as much pleasure as they on that inevitable day when the name of Thomas Sergeant Perry is, at long last, accorded just recognition and fame in the history of American culture.

To my wife, Lorna, who knows full well the joy and cost of both literary and biological labor and who also shared so willingly in the delivery of my every word, I acknowledge my permanent gratitude and affection.

THE CLEMENT VISION

I have not lost the sense of the value for me, at the time, of the admirable Russian's testimony. . . . Other echoes from the same source linger with me, I confess, as unfadingly—if it be not all indeed one much-embracing echo.

Preface, The Portrait of a Lady

One never really chooses one's general range of vision—the experience from which ideas and themes and suggestions spring: this proves ever what it has had to be, this is one with the very turn one's life has taken; so that whatever it "gives," whatever it makes us feel and think of, we regard very much as imposed and inevitable.

Preface, Lady Barberina

CHAPTER ONE

Two Provincial Realists
and the Poetry of Perception

Capping a fond recitation of the lessons he had absorbed from the "beautiful genius," Ivan Turgenev, Henry James, well into his triumphant "late phase," admitted: "Other echoes from the same source linger with me, I confess . . . if it be not all indeed one much-embracing echo." To the ear of posterity, James's tribute carries a distinct note of false modesty. For Henry James is himself a name of high repute in literary history; beyond like or dislike, he is a major figure in any reckoning of the evolution of novelistic form. Meanwhile, even alert literary minds need some reminding that during the lifetimes of James, Flaubert, and Maupassant the name of Ivan Turgenev figured large in any responsible account of literary innovation. It is everywhere apparent that Turgenev's example need no longer be cited by reputable modern annalists—or analysts—of the novel. In fact, as influential an admirer as Donald Davie has remarked that "an affection for Turgenev is recognized as evidence of a distinguished sensibility, but it has also an air slightly valetudinarian or even precious."[1] Still, Henry James's consistently high esteem for the Russian "novelists' novelist," especially in light of our current neglect or devaluation of Turgenev, would seem to call for an attentive second look. Such is the primary object of this study: to take a reading of the aesthetic and cultural impact of Turgenev's precedent upon the evolving craft of Henry James.

What will be attempted in the following pages is necessarily an "influence study" which explores beyond textual echoes. Can anyone seriously doubt that what makes a novelist initially select a particular subject is that this subject manifests a particular conduct of life that is of exemplary value to him?[2] Few scholars, I suspect, would doubt that the young Henry James frequently selected Turgenevan subjects for imaginative re-creation; this can be—and has been—demonstrated. What I investigate, what I try to demonstrate, is the *organic* conjunction of aesthetic, cultural, and temperamental leanings that made Turgenev's example, as man and artist, permanently alluring to the creative imagination of the much younger Henry James. Ultimately, I seek to locate "influence" beyond the realm of shared themes and forms, though this is what first must be brought into view. More important, I feel, is to attempt to re-view the total context in which Turgenev's significance was first perceived in America. Why should so many cultivated Americans have agreed with James that Turgenev offered a uniquely compatible and inspirational way of imagining the "felt truth" of life? In asking that question, I acknowledge that I am setting my sights to a sweeping scope of inquiry. But, for me, the venture has been worth its risks. The entire question of literary influence only interests me when it inquires into those prior mysteries of cultural and temperamental affinities which stimulate actual textual borrowings.

As I explored the Turgenev-James connection for evidence of experiential as well as artistic sympathies, I kept coming across fascinating side effects of my main inquiry. This one instance of literary kinship seemed to shed an ever more illuminating light on the reception and the refraction of nineteenth-century Realism among those cultures on the provincial periphery of Europe. More and more, the Turgenev-James relationship struck me as an instructive paradigm for comprehending some structural and narrative idiosyncracies evident in the work of nineteenth-century provincial realists. In particular, I found the now disused and vague concept of "poetic realism" taking on more concrete substance the more I observed the mutual respect the Russian and the American writer had for the poetic narratives of their German or Scandinavian or Swiss comrade realists.

It might prove helpful to resuscitate the term, "poetic realism." It is a fact that the Turgenevan and Jamesian transcriptions of life deliberately emphasize the power of human perception to extract felt value from even the most constricting and circumscribing of circumstantial realities. The aesthetic bias of both the Russian and the American realist is toward a rendition of reality that stresses the centrality of perceptual definitions of "the real." Both writers emphasize the play of perspective and the "point of view." Both favor the technique of filtering raw experience through a mediating consciousness which transvalues harsh objective contingencies in inspired leaps of redemptive perception. Both authors seem to assume that authentic realism can only exist on a perceptual, experiential base—on what might today be called a "phenomenological" grounding of truth. Beyond that, Turgenev and James are distinctive in their partiality for presenting those varieties of experience which testify to the value-creating genius of a sovereign imagination. Whether one labels the disposition of this realism "poetic" or not is a minor matter. My major concern is that an idiosyncratic and innovative species of literary realism be recognized.

The tales of experience recounted by Turgenev and James are not easily placed in our current critical topographies of Realism. Etymologically, as Harry Levin has reminded us, realism is *thing*-ism; the first definition of "real" in Johnson's Dictionary is "relating to things, not persons."[3] In accord with the primary received meaning, one would expect literary realism, in the strict sense, to denote fictional narratives which corroborate the primacy of material circumstances in the plotting of experience. And, indeed, Donald Fanger has described the stylistic aspiration of "pure" realism as "the rendering of objects in their essential quiddity."[4] Realism, strictly speaking, treats the "givens" that confront ordinary lives—and the "givenness" of a human destiny is treated with somber seriousness. Strict realism assumes the relentless narrative unfolding of a primal scene. Saul Bellow speaks directly of this archetypal plot in describing his independent rediscovery of "the essence of much of modern realism" while actually writing *The Victim*.[5]

Pit any ordinary individual—and realistic literature concerns itself with ordinary individuals—against the external world, and the external world will conquer him, of course. Everything that people believed in the 19th century about determinism, about man's place in nature, and the power of productive forces in society, made it inevitable that the hero of the realistic novel should not be a hero but a sufferer who is eventually overcome.

Certainly many critics would concur. The typical action of a realistic novel has been described as a calculated sequence of systematic disillusionments in which "the protagonist of the novel is likely to

3

discover, with Falstaff, that there is no future for heroism, that he himself is a perfectly ordinary man, with the experience and the knowledge that suit his station."[6] But if such an action may serve as a useful model for what happens in a representative nineteenth-century *Bildungsroman*, it will not serve as a useful summary of a Turgenevan or Jamesian "Novel of Apprenticeship." Protagonists like Isabel Archer or Lavretsky do undergo a systematic disillusionment, but the responsibility for their victimizations cannot be assigned unconditionally to the tyranny of objective conditions. Nor can it be claimed that such figures have been overcome irreconcilably by the brute force of fatal contingencies. The disenchanted heroes of Turgenev and James possess an imaginative vitality, a Stevensian "violence from within" that often enables them to counterbalance, or even to redeem, the violence from without. Neither the Russian nor the American would subscribe to the overdetermined plotting implicit in pure realism.

It is equally difficult, however, to place Turgenev or James in the rival camp of Romantic Realism that Donald Fanger so brilliantly discerned. The tutelary genius presiding over this school of realism is Balzac; and in Balzac what confronts the reader, as Erich Auerbach has demonstrated, is "the unity of a particular milieu, felt as a total concept of a demonic-organic nature and presented entirely by suggestive and sensory means."[7] The romantic realists themselves dominate and define any "poeticization" of reality that takes shape in their novels. They are, in Fanger's succinct phrase, "the mytho-poets of the novel,"—they are confident visionaries who suffuse an elaborately detailed, representative macrocosm with idiosyncratic highlightings and deformations dictated by their own sensibilities, by their own sense of the existential atmosphere.[8] By contrast, Turgenev and James are already postromantic in their interpretation of the prerogatives of a realistic author. They refuse to impose a unilateral settlement on their fictional renditions of experiential truth. The "poetry of perception" that arises in their realistic narratives of disillusioning experience emanates from a protagonist's sensibility and is affirmed as valid for that protagonist alone.

Turgenev and James are not romantic realists, but they do not invalidate the poetry of perception, either. They are not "pure" realists; yet they do plot anti-romances, fables of disenchantment in which experience invariably crushes the protagonist's conventional conceptualizations of life. It is my thesis that the Russian and the American make room for a clement vision of experience by grounding the possibility for redemptive aesthetic appreciations of life in a realism that insists upon the priority of perception over circumstance. This narrative strategy is special. It presents experience itself as an on-going, integrative, aesthetic process.

In the following pages I try to present a close discriminating study of the formal and temperamental affinities that link together the practice of realism in Turgenev and James. I also observe the fascinating historical correlation between an avid appreciation for poetic realism and the self-consciousness of a provincial culture. Much research needs to be done comparing provincial literatures to determine whether there is a "provincial sensibility" that innovates literary forms and structures along a shared line of bias. One of the few cultural historians to reflect upon the positive cultural contributions of provincialism is, oddly enough, Sir Kenneth Clark, whose name recently personified cosmopolitan "civilisation" in every television household. In his presidential address to the English Association in 1962, he speculated that the provinces "wish to express certain human values which the centre, with its concentration on formal values, has neglected . . . truth to nature and individual judgment. These are the recurrent catchwords of provincial art in its struggle to free itself from the dominating style."[9] Sir Kenneth's formulation has the ring of a grand generalization, but it is nonetheless stimulating. Particularly provocative is his suggestion that the self-conscious provincial artist is likely, in reaction against the technical regimentation of the ruling "metropolitan formalism," to force a legitimate place in the canon of high art for the local anecdote and the private vision. Did not the novel of poetic realism function, in effect, to force a metropolitan school to admit the substantial claims of regional and individualistic bias in defining "reality"?

Certainly the novel, in its nineteenth-century peregrinations along the periphery of Western Europe, did take on narrative mutations that made the genre even more of a hybrid than it had originally been. In Scotland, Russia, and America—to name but three instances—novelistic narratives tended to be invaded by, or interfused with, more "archaic" structurings of represented experience: Scott's "border epics," the American "romance-novel," and the Russian "family chronicle" have all become familiar classroom tags used to label some highly unusual narrative modifications that occurred in the evolution of novelistic form. In each case, the provincial novelist has regressed in his imagination away from the metropolitan bourgeois formulas for representing what is deemed a contemporary encounter with reality. At an extreme, we even get a fat Victorian novel that turns out to be the reembodiment of an authentic pastoral figure relocated in an urban setting—Goncharov's *Oblomov*. But without resorting to extremes, some idiosyncratic tendencies in the nineteenth-century provincial novel can readily be detected. The defection of the provincial author's imagination from the formal canon of the cultural center is generally manifest in the foremost works of literary realism produced outside France and England.

Especially in Russia and America we encounter articulate realists who deeply distrusted the clinical objectivity and the idolatry of the "exact word" associated with thing-oriented and sociocentric versions of representational art. Renato Poggioli has written suggestively about the stylistic distinctiveness of "The Tradition of Russian Realism" with its innate, spontaneous bias toward impressionistic, perceived valuations of the real.[10] I trust that my discussion of the first burgeonings of an American realism will suggest a clear analogue to the Russian attitudes sketched by Poggioli. And I hope that my discussion of the formal innovations achieved by Turgenev and James succeeds in drawing the reader's attention to a mutually shared cast of mind, one shaped by a provincial upbringing. Poetic realism in Turgenev and James is, I believe, the formal aesthetic embodiment of a distinctively provincial sense of reality. Their narratives knowingly, cunningly appeal to "experience" to prove that the *real* truth is, when all is said and done, a *revealed* truth of perception.

D.H. Lawrence once claimed that the whole of Russian literature was a vast attempt to perceive and to express "the phenomenal coruscations of the souls of quite commonplace people."[11] Perhaps it is in the nature of any provincial literature to insist, as do the poetic realists, upon the "phenomenal" perceptiveness of spontaneous, ingenuous souls. Perhaps provincials must be, of necessity, great believers in maintaining the worth and validity of indigenous points of view.

CHAPTER TWO

Turgenev and the
Theory of the "Dramatic" Novel

Only a short time ago it might have been supposed that the English novel was not what the French call discutable. *It had no air of having a theory, a conviction, a consciousness of itself behind it—of being the expression of an artistic faith, the result of choice and comparison.*

"The Art of Fiction" (1884)

"The era of discussion would appear to have been to a certain extent opened." On this jubilant, if understated, note of intellectual and aesthetic liberation Henry James launched forth his first major manifesto proclaiming the novel, properly conceived, "as free and as serious a branch of literature as any other." Earlier in the same year, Julian Hawthorne, a prominent opponent of the new verisimilitude in American fiction, reluctantly recognized Ivan Sergeevich Turgenev as "the novelist who, in a larger degree than any other, seems to be the literary parent of our own best men of fiction." The son of America's great "romancer" went on to refer to Turgenev's "extraordinary novels" as "altogether the most important fact in the literature of fiction of the last twelve years."[1] It was also in 1884 that William Dean Howells confidently asserted the "prevalence of realism" in the American artistic atmosphere.[2] Just two years before, Howells, in defense of Henry James, had caused a trans-Atlantic furor by challenging the tact of the British writing fraternity. "The art of fiction has, in fact, become a finer art in our day than it was with Dickens and Thackeray."[3] By the early 1880s, a militant new school of American theorists of the novel had fully emerged from the literary columns of "quality" Eastern journals such as *Atlantic Monthly* and *The Nation*.

Throughout the formative period of this prose aesthetic, the name of Ivan Turgenev was inextricably interwoven with the major threads of the new theory: "commonplace realism," "dramatic rendering," "the finest presentation of the familiar." This phenomenon presents literary

7

historians with a unique situation. In no other contemporary Western literature did the introduction of Turgenev transmit such a galvanizing theoretical impulse.[4] Why, then, should a Russian author have been the central figure in the American articulation of theories of authorial detachment and impersonality that are usually attributed to the French tradition of *écriture artiste*? Turgenev's great vogue among the proto-realists of the "genteel era" remains a neglected—and symptomatic—episode in the history of American taste.

This period was not without other glaring peculiarities, too. For instance, the select group of Eastern critics who promoted Turgenev, codified the "dramatic" novel, and emerged as the vanguard of American realism publicly manifested a clear partiality for the literary products of the cultural provinces of contemporary Europe—Scandinavia, Switzerland, Italy. It seemed almost a desideratum in itself to maintain the maximum possible aesthetic distance from both England and France. The somewhat eccentric literary preferences of the American realists offer striking evidence that a culture-specific bias had come into play as soon as modern European social fiction began to cross the Atlantic. For some reason, hinterland novelists were more exciting to the American avant-garde.

It is well to remind ourselves that the first anti-Victorians were themselves Victorians.[5] The tension contained in that paradoxical statement was much in evidence in postbellum America. On the one hand, the aftermath of a grueling internecine war brought a deep disenchantment with perfervid moralism, a revolt against sentimentalism, and a new-found willingness to entertain diversions and diversities. The age of the popular tract vanished when the nation took its toll in war casualties. Significantly, the time had now come when "Puritanism" as an epithet of honor had to be defended; it was too closely associated with the bane of aggressive sectionalism.[6] In the thriving and compendious literary monthlies of Reconstruction America a new form of popular literature arose—the travel sketch and the tale of local color. These genres reflected a growing intellectual trend toward perspectivism and a relativization of value, a trend graphically illustrated by *The Century*'s "War Series" of the 1880s in which Northern and Southern accounts of the same event were bound together.

But despite, perhaps because of, this new postwar openness to experience, a reverse current was also evident. The period was beset with an anxiety that the flux of surface diversities might render incoherent the hoped-for scenario of triumphant reunion. The Reconstruction generation was in dire need of a myth of unity which would not offend its postheroic sense of toughened realism. "In that ultimate war for Union in the American consciousness all regions and local allegiances were at odds and provided the realistic materials for a romance called the Great American Novel."[7] American realism, from its inception, was dominated by the quest for a concrete imaginative demonstration of a national society, an American Kosmos which could contain and reconcile diverse multitudes. The "National" novels of DeForest and Howells achieve this containment of dissension in different modes: the one by the romantic plot convention of cross-sectional marriage, the other by psychological assimilation and broadened sensibility. Both novelists were really recapitulating in nationalistic fictional terms America's favorite cosmology—Herbert Spencer's optimistic universe, evolving from an incoherent homogeneity toward a coherent heterogeneity. Perhaps the vast popularity of Spencer's system resulted from its providing a pseudoscientific bridge across which Americans could pass from the trauma of a divided Union into the vision of a pluralistic society.

The price of this emerging pluralism was to be a self-imposed mannerliness and gentility. The body-blow which the Civil War struck at the American sense of nationality hampered the postwar impulse to indulge an eclectic "cult of experience." It may well be true of the 1870s that "it would be hard to find a period in American history when Art (with a capital) was taken more seriously or when the aesthetic ache was stronger in the blood."[8] Americans were, indeed, seeking to compose a culture out of the shambles of the old. They displayed a new appreciation and tolerance for sectional traits and they made pilgrimages to other societies to acquire models of civilized grace. But the young generation of American taste-makers who were to articulate the standards of the postbellum prose aesthetic feared alike the extremes of nativism and cosmopolitanism. The thrust of their critical enterprise was to redefine the American character as an attitude, a stance, a decorum that one maintained amid the flux of *faits divers*. They were especially concerned to keep this hard-won American perspective free from being overborne by the weighty cultural authority of English "didacticism" or French "paganism." As Gordon Haight has observed, American realism was not a frontier phenomenon; all our early artistic realists earned their spurs as "back trailers, thrown by circumstance into an older, more sophisticated society."[9] But, caught between the rival aesthetics of the English and the French, and seeking an equilibrium between moral meaning and aesthetic integrity, the Americans found it less humiliating and more natural to acknowledge a public debt to the poetic realism developed in the more rural provinces of European culture.[10] In culture, as in finance, it is apparently less hurtful to one's pride to borrow from one's social peers or inferiors.

At first glance, the young Henry James would seem to be the special case that belies that generalization. Recalling his earliest impression of James, whom he first met in 1866, William Dean Howells mentioned that "James was inveterately and intensely French ... He could not always keep his French background back, and sometimes he wrote English that was easily convicted of Gallicism."[11] But if, as Mario Praz has wittily noted, Delacroix's painting, *La Liberté guidant le peuple*, could be taken as an emblem of the French spirit in the nineteenth century, then Henry James spoke for another France.[12] There were, to be sure, isolated Americans who did bathe in the latest libertarian currents from France like the painter-essayist, Eugene Benson. Benson was a proto-Mencken waging a one-man *fronde* for the "pagan element" against the "preachy-teachy-prosy" proprieties of Anglo-Saxondom in the pages of New York's *Galaxy*. This campaign, which lasted from 1866 to 1869, ended when the editors gave Benson a parting public drubbing. But the France in which the young James was steeped was not the France of Bohemia, nor even the France of *Bovary*. At the time of his critical debut in 1864, the core struggle in James between his "English wholesomeness" and his "artistic subtlety" guided him into the conservative camp of French criticism associated with the bulky and staid *Revue des Deux Mondes*.[13]

Later in life Henry James fondly recalled the image of himself as a young and restive repatriate in Newport paying his respects to the thick pink *Revues* "as the very headspring of culture, a mainstay in exile."[14] It was in the quiet antebellum summer of 1858 that the seeds of a new American art of fiction had been sown. For the precocious adolescent James was not alone in closeting himself with the tomes of the *Revue*. He had the companionship of an even more precocious Newport prodigy, one of the most voracious book-lovers on the contemporary scene, Thomas Sergeant Perry.[15] Together these two arbiters of the future of the American novel absorbed the critical predispositions of the *Revue des Deux Mondes*.

This journal, which was known as a bastion of "idealism" in art, had been circulating in America since the early 1840s, enjoying great prestige, especially among the Transcendentalists.[16] It had been moving

10

with the general tendency of French taste after 1830 in reacting against the extravagant imbroglios of the novel of incident, favoring instead the more circumscribed novel of analysis—the *roman intime*.[17] But while championing the novel of character, the leading critics of the *Revue* were very much classical in their preference for generalized, typological studies and in their bias against Balzac's immersion of character in the toils of special milieux.[18] Gustave Planche, in fact, was largely responsible for the confusion of literary realism with literalism, or the exact imitation *(calque)* of nature as it is, without choice of subject, without idealization and intrusion of the artist's personality.[19] At about the time of the Newport readings, however, a major shift in sensibility was under way. Largely in response to the serialization of *Madame Bovary* in 1856, the *Revue* began making concessions to less impassive and "physiological" varieties of realism—a movement which culminated in the publication of Hippolyte Taine's articles canonizing Balzac.[20] Even so, the most highly acclaimed prose artist in the canon of the *Revue* was unquestionably Prosper Mérimée, with his unique combination of classical restraint and order with a picturesque, exotic realism.[21] Through their literary nursemaid, the *Revue*, James and Perry thus acquired the palate for a cool and composed "high style" realism that would be artistic without being either sentimental or surgical.

Early in the summer of 1859, the Newport camaraderie suddenly expanded into an aesthetic coterie. The studio of William Morris Hunt, which had already drawn William James into apprenticeship, now lured a most seductive, vivid specimen of Continental polish. The dashing Franco-American painter, John LaFarge, struck the impressionable Henry James as "an embodiment of the gospel of aesthetics." "Out of the safe rich home of the *Revue*, which opened away into the vastness of visions, he practically stepped."[22] This new arrival literally forged a blood link between the Newport novices and the literary salons of Paris. LaFarge, who had been in France in 1856, was cousin to Paul de Saint-Victor, a former secretary to Lamartine and intimate of Gautier. In 1860, in a symbolic union of the deracinated, John LaFarge wed Margaret Perry, the eldest sister of T. S. Perry. Ease of intercourse between Europeanized Americans and Americanized Europeans was fast becoming a reality. In the remaining few seasons of Henry James's Newport idyll, John LaFarge served as a living supplement to the *Revues*. Taking Perry and the James brothers aside, he explicated Balzac and gave proper entrée into "the square and dense little formal

11

garden of Mérimée.'' LaFarge was also very articulate about his commitment to the theories and techniques of that school of dignified and earthy landscape associated with J. F. Millet. Keeping in mind the close historical connection between pronouncements of literary realism and defenses of the craft of "low" representational art, we ought not to forget LaFarge's contribution in training the "painter's eye" of two great American theorists of the novel.[23] Henry James and T. S. Perry were exposed in Newport to LaFarge's own experiments in point-of-view: ". . . studies out of the window to give the effect and appearance of *looking out* of the window and our not being in the same light as the landscape."[24] Surely it was no mean accomplishment, in mid-century New England, to have conveyed, as LaFarge did, the art of the nuance.

The advent of the Civil War would seem scarcely to have touched the aesthetic foundations on which James and Perry were building. Both entered Harvard in 1862 and quietly continued to school themselves in the decorous opposition to sentimentality and sensationalism favored by the conservative French criticism. James, in true gentlemanly fashion, was "perfectly and properly vague" about his abortive law studies while avidly immersing himself in Sainte-Beuve at the Gore Hall Library. Ultimately he emerged as a brash young recruit in Charles Eliot Norton's cultural warfare against the gushing, formless romances of the many American lady writers. Perry compiled only a middling record as a scholar while pursuing with congenital gusto his own private elective of "deep researches into novels."[25] These years of wide-ranging and, from an academic standpoint, fashionable readings did, however, produce crucial shifts in taste. In the immediate postwar period, James and Perry stepped forward bearing the banner of new Continental critics with new standards for the novel. And in their selection of guides, the subtle pressure of Reconstruction anxieties can be sensed.

Meditating on his glimpse of the tattered Union legions recuperating at Portsmouth Grove, Henry James movingly recorded the shock, on American ground, of "the recognition, by any sensibility at all reflective, of the point where our national theory of absorption, assimilation, and conversion appallingly breaks down."[26] This shattering experience opened a painful intellectual breach through which new currents of relativism could flow. One aspect of this growing acceptance of the tentative can be seen in James's appreciation for the methodology of the literary portrait as practised by Sainte-Beuve, with its anxiety to preserve intact the fleeting and authentic impressions made on a recording consciousness.[27] But as regards the novel in particular, the beginnings of a new orientation can be dated from James's first tribute of 1865 in *The Nation* to Edmond Scherer. "The philosopher's function is to compare a work with an abstract principle of truth; the critic's is to compare a work with itself, with its own concrete standard of truth."[28] What made Scherer so attractive to James was his healthy eclecticism, his willingness to entertain varieties of expression without imposing any "outer servitude" in the form of a literary canon. It was precisely this undogmatic delight in the "plastic force of life" that had first brought Scherer a degree of notoriety. He attained prominence with an article on Hegelianism which appeared in the *Revue des Deux Mondes* in 1861. In the article Scherer spoke of the validity of context in a bold manner foreshadowing a much later Henry James. "It is . . . not enough to say: everything is only relative; we must add: everything is only relation."[29] Yet despite this unabashed relativism, Scherer anchored his critical standards in the consistency of his own moral conscience. This, too, had its inevitable appeal to an American postwar generation whose ethical absolutes had become unmoored.

Edmond Scherer offered a model of adjustment to an age that had outlived ideologies. He had weathered his own crisis of faith. Originally a Swiss Calvinist theologian, he had defected from the dogma under the impact of German historicism. But he had responded to the pressures of incertitude by formulating a humane cult of decency and manners— what he liked to call "the art of life."[30] As James so well expressed it, Scherer, who abhorred obtrusive moralizing, nonetheless offered a reassuring example of "that wisdom which, after having made the journey round the whole sphere of knowledge, returns at last with a melancholy joy to morality."[31] Given this strong intellectual empathy, it is not surprising that James in his novelistic criticism of the 1870s should so often have treated the same subjects and reached similar conclusions with Scherer.[32] Following in Scherer's wake, James used his new-found respect for contextual truth to chart a middle course in narrative technique between the twin complacencies of didacticism and clinical objectivity. The emancipated Swiss Calvinist proved a reliable pilot to a later James, navigating his craft between George Eliot and Gustave Flaubert. Scherer's influence helped to push aside absolute certitude and give elbowroom for the new categories of the complex, the ambivalent, and the viable.

All during this postwar period, Henry James had a direct source of supply for Continental novelties through his old schoolmate, T. S. Perry. Immediately after graduation from Harvard in 1866, Perry had embarked on a combination grand tour, graduate-school-abroad program that lasted two years and covered much of western Europe. From October 1867, into the following year, "Sarge" Perry lived and studied in Berlin with William James, who had left Cambridge to acquire a competence in German behavioral psychology. For brother Henry, it was a cruel reversal of roles with Perry; *he* was now the sedentary stay-at-home scholar. In his letters he complained often of the lack of satisfactory society, decent literature, and general "delectation" in Cambridge.[33] But the reverse flow of letters was filled with solid literary nutriment. Even before Perry's arrival in Berlin, William had reported a two-month "debauch" on French fiction, during which he especially relished the "golden-mouthed" clarity of Gautier's travel sketches and the witty complications in the prose comedies of the now-neglected Swiss author, Victor Cherbuliez.[34] Once Henry's "super-excellent and all-reading" friend had arrived, a lively exchange and comparison of notes on novelists was begun. The excitement bred by the Continental novelties they discussed was well conveyed in one of Perry's later journalistic salvos. "In our novels we pay for their innocence by too many pale, passionless figures . . . A novelist, like everyone else, should avoid prudishness; and we could pray that English-writing authors, while they still retain their present ground of moral dignity . . . learn some of the methods of their French brethren."[35] In the eventual literary campaign to admit the passional element while retaining the ethical, we should note the centrality for Americans of the Geneva-born Cherbuliez, about whom Perry was to write nine reviews and two extended articles. The Swiss author impressed Americans with the detached sobriety of his narrative manner. To be sure, he wrote of sexual folly, but with a "wider cultivation" than did the Parisians. He shunned both the gross effects of melodrama and the temptation to deliver affidavits rather than present scenes. In short, Cherbuliez distinguished himself from his French rivals by treating risqué topics from a highly intellectualized, comedy-of-manners stance.[36] Sophisticated and genteel Americans, like Perry, were learning from hinterland Europeans, like Cherbuliez, to employ civilized wit as a device for broaching matters otherwise too delicate for native standards of public discussion.

T. S. Perry's broad acquaintance with the Continental literary scene was probably the single most important factor in precipitating an American theory of the dramatic novel. In Germany Perry discovered a critic who nicely complemented Scherer's tastes, while avoiding the extremity of his philosophical relativism. In retrospect, the American discussion of a "poetic realism" and of Turgenev's vital relevance to it can be seen as deriving from the essays of Julian Schmidt. Schmidt, who was co-editor with Gustav Freytag of the Vienna *Grenzboten* (1842-82) and a close associate of agrarian realists like Berthold Auerbach and Fritz Reuter, gained an American audience through his critical essays in the monumental, four-volume *Pictures from the Spiritual Life of Our Time* (1870-75). A political liberal, he saw himself as "the defender of the public taste as against literary exclusiveness" and urged the German artist to "seek the people at its labor."[37] His importance to Americans was twofold. First, he was a sympathetic Continental advocate of the "moderate realism" he detected in English fiction from Scott to George Eliot. Second, he interpreted the original genius of Turgenev for the Western reader; the French, with the notable exception of Mérimée, did not devote themselves to a major critical investigation of the Russian writer.[38]

A great admirer of *Adam Bede*, Schmidt sought to cure the German penchant for lofty theorizing with a healthy injection of "the faithful representing of commonplace things." For Schmidt, like George Eliot, the adjective "faithful" in that context implied a whole ethic of good-natured tolerance for the mixed characters inhabiting a finite world. Schmidt's advocacy of moderate or poetic realism also contained a hidden rural bias. Citing Scott's example in *The Heart of Midlothian*, he encouraged the writing of extended *Dorfgeschichten*, or village tales, in which episodes involving intergroup relations would reveal the natural geniality arising from the relaxed pace of country life.[39] Whereas Scherer had proclaimed "everything is relation," Schmidt might have declared "toleration is all." The latter was a more comfortable working premise for postbellum Americans to adopt. Although an Anglophile, Schmidt also managed to assuage the pangs of cultural inferiority to which provincials are so prone. Perry, for one, was much impressed by Schmidt's criticism of the "lumbering, inartistic form" typical of the English novelist, who "draws his characters with great fullness, and then drifts through a sea of incidents without any clearly conceived plan, and ends his story much more according to the demands of the book-seller than according to the necessities of a dramatic plot."[40] As we shall see, it was Julian Schmidt who first saw Turgenev as the finest exemplar of a poetic realism that could be both aesthetically and ethically balanced. It was a lead the American critics were not long in following.

The Clement Vision

In the autumn of 1868, T. S. Perry returned to Cambridge with his added stores of erudition. Soon afterward, he and other Harvardians founded "The Club," where the "best conversation" in Boston was exchanged for nearly sixty years; among the fourteen charter members were the brothers James and William Dean Howells.[41] Howells, now on the threshold of his brilliant career as editor of *Atlantic Monthly*, had been settling the true principles of literary art in sessions with Henry James since 1866. He certainly was aware of the literary tendencies that were now in the air. In later life, he frankly acknowledged that Perry had taught him "the new and true way of looking at literature."[42] This admission bears repeating because Perry himself did not enter the lists of journalism until 1871, and some critics have tended to inflate Howells's contribution to the formulation of the postwar theory of the novel.[43] What is clear is that 1869 was the year of the first public airing for the new winds of doctrine. Both in Boston and New York, a minor critical boom for German *Dorfgeschichten*, and especially for Berthold Auerbach, was initiated.[44] And Howells, in his review of *Edelweiss*, gave the first intimation that new demands were to be made on narrative artists. The primary charm of the story, Howells said, was that it told itself: "From the beginning it *goes alone*."[45]

A true frontal attack on the stale conventions of Anglo-American prose did not materialize until April 1870. Then, in what has been called the first concise statement of his theory of fiction, Howells presented the Norwegian "romances" of Bjornstjerne Bjornson as a needed "escape from the jejune inventions and stock repetitions of what really seems a failing art to us."[46] Like Schmidt in Germany, Howells was launching an offensive against the novel of melodramatic incident, against the kind of "plottiness" that imposed an alien order on life. Howells's article expressed the reaction against "all that is Trollopian in literary art"—the swarm of petty details, the obtrusive authorial generalizations, the clash of extreme positions, the caprices of phrase. It asserted that American writers would do well to emulate the artists of hinterland Europe, those who had faith in the reader's ability to respond, unprodded, to natural beauty, and who demonstrated that "the finest poetry is not ashamed of the plainest fact." Oddly enough, the type of novel which should appeal to the cultural ideals of the American democrat was being written in Europe. Accordingly, Howells's first change as editor-in-chief of *Atlantic* was to institute a department of "Recent Literature" which gave generous space to

Turgenev and the Theory of the "Dramatic" Novel

French and German publications. The chosen steward of this new foreign section was T. S. Perry. Very rapidly a Turgenev cult sprang up in America.

What seems most striking today is not the cult itself, but the delay in the American critical response to Turgenev. Translations and reviews of the Russian's works had been appearing in the *Revue des Deux Mondes* since 1854. "Tourguéneff" was surely one of those Continental novelties secreted in the Newport closet of 1858. Positive proof of an early acquaintance with the Russian can be found in a letter from William to Henry James in 1869 praising the style and artistry of the *Nouvelles moscovites* by "your old friend Turgénieff."[47] Even beyond the cosmopolitan James circle, Turgenev was no stranger to the cultured American readership. Russia's support of the Union and the roughly contemporary emancipations of serfs and slaves had produced a wave of sympathetic interest in Russian culture. In 1867 Eugene Schuyler, the future diplomat, produced an excellent American translation of *Fathers and Children*. Why, then, did American recognition of Turgenev's aesthetic significance have to await 1871 and the debut of T. S. Perry as foreign reviewer for *Atlantic* and *The Nation*? It is very likely that American critics lacked the confidence to tread where European aestheticians had not yet paved the way. Perry's daring assertion that Turgenev, as a stylist, was "at the head of living novelists" was unquestionably borrowed from Julian Schmidt's collected essays of 1870.[48] In short, Schmidt's extensive evaluation of Turgenev provided the European imprimatur under which an American cult could flourish.

It was Schmidt who propagated the now familiar contrast between Turgenev's *Sportsman's Sketches* and *Uncle Tom's Cabin*, pointing out the superior affective impact of objective rendering and selective detail over authorial rhapsodizing and sentimentality. It was Schmidt who hailed Turgenev's lifelike representation of character, achieved through the presentation of significant gesture in place of lengthy narrative analysis. And it was Schmidt who placed Turgenev in the forefront of a modern poetic realism. The German critic realized that Turgenev had built an aesthetic component into his very concept of physical reality. In a later essay, Schmidt referred to Turgenev, the author of realistic novels of manners, as fundamentally a "genre poet." Much as a genre painter imposes a cast of mind, a coloration of mood upon an empirically observable scene, so Turgenev possessed the talent to infuse

17

a value-charged perspective, a private point of view, into a long narrative sequence dealing with quotidian life: "he depicts only what he deems will expedite the creation of a harmonious, integral canvas."[49]

Beginning in 1871 with Perry's access to the leading cultural journals, these sophisticated attitudes toward Turgenev were broadcast among Eastern intellectuals. Like Schmidt, Perry announced his preference for Turgenev's artistic realism as opposed to Balzac's microscopic realism; the Russian, "always a narrator, never an advocate," wisely avoided the obtrusive melodrama and the intrusive clinical analysis of the French manner.[50] Taking a cue from Mérimée, Perry also stressed Turgenev's extreme respect for the individuation of character and destiny—deliberately eschewing conventional types and happy terminations, the Russian left readers "perplexed as we are in real life." Perry's criticism, with its militant insistence on the necessary finitude of the authorial vision, advanced Turgenev as the exemplar of the well-made, realistic novel of manners.

By 1874 the moment was at hand for the canonization of Ivan Turgenev as the patron saint of the American theory of the dramatic novel. The indefatigable Perry had extended his influence as far afield as *Lippincott's* of Philadelphia, New York's *Galaxy*, and the Brahmin precincts of the *North American Review*.[51] Through his close association with Perry, Howells began granting superlatives to Turgenev as the most impartial narrator among the story-telling tribe. In December 1873, direct contact with the Russian author was established through a strange intermediary—the Norwegian-American novelist, Hjalmar Hjorth Boyesen.[52] This expatriated Swedenborgian journalist and purveyor of Norse sagas had stumbled across Howells's path in Cambridge in 1871. Howells was then at the height of his enthusiasm for Bjornson. The two quickly established a comfortable working relationship, Howells exchanging editorial advice to the neophyte author for accurate information on Bjornson. Howells also communicated to Boyesen his new-found enthusiasm for Julian Schmidt and Ivan Turgenev. In 1873 when Boyeson was offered summer leave from Cornell to visit the European literary scene, it was only natural for this ambitious journalist to enrich his contacts. Through Julian Schmidt's letter of introduction, he interviewed Turgenev in Paris. The resultant anecdotal essay, "A Visit to Tourguéneff," served to confirm the aesthetic speculations made by Perry about the Russian.[53] Boyesen's conversational vignette of the author Schmidt thought to be "perhaps the greatest now living" must have lifted the morale of aspiring

American artists. Turgenev, in this visit, revealed not only a knowledge-able and sympathetic interest in American literature, but also the democratic presuppositions of his own characterology. Against Carlyle's doubts, he avowed a faith that individuals would always render life "motley, varied, and even disorderly." Fitting Perry's specifications, Turgenev revealed his approach to fictional portraiture as empirical and tentative, renouncing philosophical abstraction and pure imagination. "I endeavor not to give undue prominence to any one trait; even if ever so characteristic, I try to show my men and women *en face* as well as *en profile*." In conclusion, Boyesen drew the shrewd moral that if the vast, culturally barren steppes of Russia could yield up Turgenev's striking figures, then American society ought to reject the prejudice that "the mobile, ever-billowing surface of our life is unfavorable to artistic effects." The call for an American Turgenev had been sounded.

Close upon the heels of Boyesen's revelation, in June and September of 1874, came a remarkable series of articles that codified once and for all the place of Turgenev and the "dramatic method" in the evolution of the genre of the novel. The incipient American realists had lacked a critic with the synoptic breadth to place their creative impulses in the context of the international development of the novel. Now a hitherto unfeatured writer, the associate editor of *Atlantic*, German-educated George Parsons Lathrop, produced two programmatic statements on the growth and the future of the novel. Ironically, the son-in-law of Nathaniel Hawthorne was to construct the theoretical bridge which allowed passage from the American romance to the new American novel.

Lathrop's first article cogently argued that all progress toward narrative verisimilitude lay in the direction of dramatic presentation.[54] Since the novel's proper sphere was the surface of life, the appearances of things, the modern novel would have to accommodate itself to the relativist, comparativist epistemology of the present. "The secret of dramatic effect is simply this, that in real life ultimate truth seldom finds a pure utterance ... [t]he involved truths of the whole proceeding being illustrated by the partial expressions of each individual." Thus, the truly modern writer would have to regard each human being as an undetermined quantity; the imposition of a mechanical moralizing would only provoke smiles. Basing himself on this conviction, Lathrop proceeded to denigrate those authors who indulged in a narrative technique founded on the discredited model of omniscience. Thack-eray, like Fielding, was too fond of winking behind the scenes in comic

19

digressions. And George Eliot, with her minute and deliberate analyses, "presides too watchfully." But Turgenev was the model for dramatic technique; he realized that narrative impersonality must not imply the lack of a distinctive style. Ideally, authorial self-renunciation must not mean invisibility or lack of control, "but only inofficiousness."

Lathrop's second pronouncement was an extraordinary anticipation of the mature Jamesian point-of-view theory.[55] Beginning with the assumption that "the novel is a portable drama," Lathrop saw the novel's superiority in its potential for a centrality of focus. "It is thus fitted to exhibit the hero as the recipient of impressions only—concentrating in him the phantasmagoric elaboration of all surrounding life through his individual senses and perceptions." Even so, the modern dramatic novel, while renouncing intervention by the authorial voice, need not, indeed must not, renounce the permeation of the fiction by the creator's views. Writing is original only inasmuch as it reflects the abiding peculiarities of the author's point of view. For Lathrop, truly realistic novels will observe this rule. The crucial realm of private values will be integrated into empirical narratives through the dramatization of "psychological phenomena." In a capsule definition, "realism sets itself at work to consider characters and events which are apparently the most ordinary and uninteresting, in order to extract from these their full value and true meaning." Thus, American realists, if Lathrop had his way, would not exclude or ignore the felt validity of human norms. Instead, the ruling authorial consciousness would structure a dramatic rendering of the mundane becoming rife with significance. In this respect, Turgenev's formal technique of narration was, in Lathrop's view, the harbinger of future novelistic practice. And although he found the Russian too chary in applying the brush of optimism, Lathrop still could conclude that "of all eminently realistic novelists, Turgénieff is . . . the most vigorous, acute, and delicate." After such definitive praise, there could be little doubt that it was Turgenev who revealed 'life' most satisfactorily to the new school of American realists.[56] As Howells admitted to Joyce Kilmer in 1914, Turgenev opened to the whole *Atlantic* circle "a new world—and it was the only real world."[57]

The real world which Turgenev opened to a generation of American prose theorists was, not surprisingly, a country of the mind very like their own. "Life" had become a protracted dramatic conflict between the valid counter-claims of the call to beauty and the call to duty. As its name implies, the American Reconstruction was an era filled with profound cultural anxieties. Two clashing imperatives met head-on: the need for an end to ideology and the quest for a reconstituted national purpose. The revolutionary nineteenth-century concept of the multiplicity of truth began to make deep inroads among American intellectuals precisely at a point in time when the American sense of nationality was most beleaguered.[58] It is against the backdrop of this cultural trauma of simultaneous relativization of value and resurgent nationalism that the vast American appeal of Ivan Sergeevich Turgenev can best be appreciated.

The aesthetic accolades Americans showered on Turgenev as the supreme mentor of the dramatic novel served mainly to mask an extensive borrowing of French narrative strategies. Turgenev's true contribution to the American innovators lay elsewhere. He offered a prototype of the provincial *Bildungsroman* that was eminently *discutable* in cosmopolitan circles. For Turgenev's dramatically-rendered character studies were, in essence, dramatizations of the plight of the provincial consciousness as it struggled to accommodate its thirst for experience with indigenous moral sensitivities. This was a narrative model which spoke directly to the felt anxieties of Reconstruction intellectuals who were equally wary of Anglo-Saxon morality and French license. It was Turgenev's "middle course" which helped a generation of Americans to define realism as a function of a given culture's point of view. And no one understood this better than Henry James.

CHAPTER THREE

Henry James and the "Beautiful Genius"

We value most the 'realists' who have an ideal of delicacy and the elegiasts who have an ideal of joy.

"Ivan Turgéniew" (1874)

it is his Russian savor that as much as anything has helped generally to domesticate him.

"Turgénieff" (1897)

Close watchers of American literary trends might well agree with William Dean Howells that Henry James's first public pronouncement on Ivan Turgenev "comes near being a masterpiece of criticism."[1] The James essay is doubly rich; it manages to be aesthetically perceptive about Turgenev while revealing some pertinent biases of American taste. Not surprisingly, it appeared first in the *North American Review* in 1874, that *annus mirabilis* for Turgenev's American reputation. On the mere evidence of its publication date, James's essay must be seen as part of the concerted campaign by young Eastern critics to promote some exemplary texts to assist the burgeoning of an American literary realism. But unlike the other American partisans of the dramatic novel, James was much less transparently *using* Turgenev as an ethically acceptable instructor in advanced narrative technique. He was not appreciative of Turgenev in order the better to propagate the methodology of a whole literary school. It is true that James helped fire the enthusiasm for a Turgenev cult by gathering together some kindling rhetoric about the Russian's mastery of dramatic form, but his appraisal was not exclusively, nor even predominantly, based on formal criteria. Despite the later James's reputation as a "formalist" literary critic, his early piece on Turgenev is distinct from other contemporary American evaluations of that writer for its emphasis on the cultural determinants of theme and character-portrayal.[2] In short, Henry James's first statement on Ivan Turgenev engaged the young American's cultural and moral, as well as his aesthetic, imagination. Turgenev elicited, as no

23

other author save perhaps George Eliot could, James's earliest speculations as to what might constitute a viable "world-view."[3]

If, as is claimed, the young Henry James was drawn toward Turgenev
for reasons more subtle than an apprenticeship in literary architec-
tonics, how can the alleged complex attraction be made manifest? One
obvious answer would be to undertake a close scrutiny of all James's
recorded comments on Turgenev. But preferences are exercised options
that emerge out of a context of multiple choices. In isolation, James's
most thoughtful and polished sentiments about Turgenev cannot begin
to convey the complex play of an uncommitted mind before a broad
field of possibility. Fortunately for us, James did embed his admiring
essay of 1874 in a dense context of entertained alternatives—the
Turgenev piece was strategically relocated in the critical collection of
1878, *French Poets and Novelists*. The binding together of James's
Turgenev with Gallic company is more than a symbolic gesture; in so
doing, James's volume restores the implicit comparisons and cross
references that comprised the field of choice out of which his
evaluation of the Russian arose. It is on the evidence of *French Poets
and Novelists* that we can best see *why* Turgenev exercised such a
strong appeal on James. We can also judge how the quality of James's
response differed from that of Turgenev's more ostentatious champions
in America.

It is easy to lose sight of how provocative a book James's first
collection of critical essays was. It is easy to exaggerate the fastidiousness James displays when confronted with Baudelaire's subject matter
and to speak glibly of a residual Puritanism informing the book's
literary standards. But as sympathetic a contemporary as Howells
sensed, with a good deal of agitation, a totally opposite tendency
permeating the collection. Howells faulted James for "a want of some
positive or negative result clearly enunciated"; James's whole attitude,
Howells felt, "implies a certain nervousness that if he curtails his
contradictory impressions he may not appear liberal enough."[4] To
American peers, James's book was clearly and disturbingly latitudinari-
an; the young critic seemed all too willing to suspend normative
judgments for too long. Yet later commentators on the early James
have equated his reactions to French art with the general current of
opinion among the Eastern realists: one might be attracted to the
technical dexterity and sensuous detail achieved by the French, while
being repelled by their lack of moral and intellectual insight.[5] The
logical extension of this line of argument would be to seek out a

compromise candidate, an author whose form was just French enough, but whose content was just British enough, to please. Turgenev is generally conceded to have been that perfect nominee. There is enough truth in this standard resumé to make it persuasive. But surely it is also simplistic and especially insensitive when applied to the young James. *French Poets and Novelists* reveals a sensibility that is attracted to French models for more than technically artistic reasons. It also reveals a sensibility too discriminating to entertain the notion of settling for a compromise solution to problems of the artistic representation of reality. Henry James both admired French tendencies and exalted Turgenev's artistry with more enthusiasm than has generally been recognized.

The first thing that ought to be said about the essays in the 1878 edition is that they are consciously addressed to an Anglo-Saxon readership and that they self-consciously announce a willingness to make "allowances."[6] And while it is true that most of the articles do eventuate in a balanced account of credits and debits, it is not accurate to imply that James closely budgets his store of enthusiasm. It is instructive to observe the sort of verbal coin he uses to pay out his debt to French artists. Again and again, James singles out for praise that aspect of a given author's work which includes, and gives aesthetic expression to, a dimension of "experience" hitherto slighted in literature. Over and over, James is urging the Anglo-Saxon reader to indulge any art that promises, in the book's implicit metaphor, to "broaden one's horizons." What makes de Musset valuable is his gift for expressing the sort of emotion which life's conventions and proprieties leave vague, "yet which forms a part of human nature important enough to have its exponent." (20) "The greatest thing in Balzac," we are told, is Balzac himself, the man as method, "that huge, all-encompassing, all-desiring, all-devouring love of reality." (116) Of a very different sort of artist, George Sand, a similar rhetoric of praise is invoked: "The determination to address herself to life at first hand—this personal, moral impulse, which was not at all a literary impulse—was her great inspiration . . . the most interesting thing about her." (160) Without adducing further examples, a reprimand to the view that James sought to divorce the form from the content of contemporary French art is in order.

Ultimately, what most attracted young Henry James to French poets and novelists was not this or that school or specific technique. It was the over-all "scope of life" reflected in French literature that James found seductive. His book of essays embodies the dramatic quest of a scrupulous sensibility eagerly pushing at the limits of experience. English literature is frankly indicted for failing to take an honest measure of "life."[7] Cautiously, James entertains the possibility of alternative French methods of measurement. "A 'high standard' is an excellent thing; but we sometimes fancy it takes away more than it gives, and that an untamed natural faculty of enjoying at a venture is a better conductor of aesthetic light and heat." (42) Especially in the virtually reverent essay on Gautier, James conveys the liberating joy he experiences when material existence can be articulated in a carefully chiseled artistic shape. One senses in the tone of that essay a wistful regret that all experience could not be purely physical and hence easily rendered shapely. Is there, so early in James's career, the daring hope that *all* experience can be given an aesthetic envelope? Might not one of his leitmotifs in this first collection of essays be "if you only look at it closely, everything is remunerative"? (44)

But if Henry James was exhilarated by the openness to experience, the sheer quantity of life, the "love of reality" exemplified in contemporary French literature, how was it that he found it impossible to commend unqualifiedly a single exemplary talent from among the French? Significantly, James finds himself discontented with all available Gallic models through the stringent application of the same criteria by which he found French artists in general superior to their Anglo-Saxon rivals. Although the French possessed the knack for importing some very alluring and unBritish dimensions of experience into literature, they, too, failed to convey, to James's specifications, the fullest illusion of "felt life."[8] De Musset, for all the sweetness and spontaneity of his verbalized passion, regrettably lived and wrote within a "contented smallness of horizon." (4) Of Gautier, that superb verbal sculptor of life's backdrops and surfaces, James sadly conceded, "our author's really splendid development is inexorably circumscribed." (55) The great Balzac, despite his sharklike appetite for seizing whatever moves, himself hunts human nature within special preserves. In fact, he epitomizes "the French passion for completeness, for symmetry, for making a system as neat as an epigram—its intolerance of the indefinite, the unformulated." (81) And even George Sand, the charming literary skylark warbling so tunefully and unpremeditatedly, turns out to be an unwittingly systematic sentimentalist. She is deficient in novelistic exactitude, "that tender appreciation of actuality which makes even the application of a single coat of rose-colour seem an act of violence."

Henry James and the "Beautiful Genius"

(185) It is against this densely-woven fabric of critical commentary that James's first essay on Turgenev proves so illuminating. In the 1878 frame, the 1874 silhouette of Turgenev's features is exposed to best advantage. In the right setting, the young James's image of his fellow cosmopolite and fellow provincial instructed him how to picture "life," "experience," and "reality." The impatient, sophisticated American eagerly glimpsed the possibility of expanding his literary panorama of life's horizon. For Turgenev, as he later expressed it, "had, with that great tradition of ventilation of the Russian mind, windows open into distances which stretched far beyond the *banlieue*."[9]

Of all the pieces collected together in the 1878 volume, the essay on Turgenev is the only one self-consciously addressed to an *American* audience and it is the only one in which James seriously worries the question of an author's feel for life. These two distinctions are distinctly interrelated. Turgenev, James senses, writes out of a poet's quarrel with an emergent nationhood; his writings portray a national character in process of formation, still in solution. Turgenev observes the awkward leaps of cultural transition with a judicious fairness. So, if the ganglingly adolescent American culture were to produce a "native novelist of a large pattern," the precedent of Turgenev would prove appropriate to the case. Implicit in James's prophecy here is the notion that unsettled, transitional, or weakly institutionalized societies encourage an ultra-comprehensive receptivity to the components of experience. Certainly the distinctive feature of the Russian author, the feature that makes him so extraordinarily relevant to James's America, is the undogmatic, synoptic quality of his rendered vision of life. From James's American perspective, Turgenev carries off the honors for conveying the impression of lifelikeness. He offers "a view of the great spectacle of human life more general, more impartial, more unreservedly intelligent than that of any novelist we know ... for 'life' in his pages is very far from meaning a dreary liability to sordid accidents, as it seems to mean with those writers of the grimly pathetic school who cultivate sympathy to the detriment of comprehension."[10] The very intensity of this praise invites a central question: what *is* the meaning of life in James's pages on Turgenev?

Conveying the illusion of life in a fictional narration is not, for James, simply a matter of projecting a "representational" plot. The trick lies primarily in the "presentational" accuracy of achieved motivation. What truly distinguishes Turgenev amidst the great company of nineteenth-century realists is his steady focus on complex, opaque subjects, "his object is constantly the same—that of finding an incident, a person, a situation, morally interesting." (217) Superior to his contemporaries, Turgenev's finely rendered surfaces reflect the agitation of problematic depths.

> In susceptibility to the sensuous impressions of life—to colours and odours and forms, and the myriad ineffable refinements and enticements of beauty—he equals, and even surpasses, the most accomplished representatives of the French school of story-telling; and yet he has, on the other hand, an apprehension of man's religious impulses, of the ascetic passion, the capacity of becoming dead to colours and odours and beauty, never dreamed of in the philosophy of Balzac and Flaubert. (219)

A recognition of man's "ascetic passion," subjects "morally interesting"—if such virtues are required to infuse fiction with life, then life is a corollary of the dramatic presentation of felt character. And if James was attracted to Turgenev for a single technical excellence, then surely it was because of the Russian's characterology. Indeed, one could virtually claim that Henry James was seduced by Turgenev's young Russian heroines.[11] We know that James was affronted by the conventionally sophisticated portrayal of feminine wiles, which he took to be coarse and reductionist. For instance, the "great sign" of Balzac's women was that "the sexual quality is inordinately emphasized and the conscience on the whole inordinately sacrificed to it. It is an idea familiar to all novelists—it is indeed half their stock in trade—that women in good and in evil act almost exclusively from personal motives." (109-10) How could the young American critic *not* resent motivational clichés about women when he knew of the moral possibility of an ingenuous, virginal venturesomeness toward experience that both charmed and maddened him in the company of his female compatriots?[12] Only in Turgenev could James find portrayals consistent with his sense of the variety and complexity of life-subjects. Apparently the Muscovite imagination also was broad enough to conceive of "original" iconoclastic young ladies who yet could exude a "touch of the faintly acrid perfume of the New England temperament— a hint of Puritan angularity . . . who mainly represent strength of will—the power to resist, to wait, to attain." (230) Apparently it took sophisticated provincials to ferret out the full array of paradoxical volitions that could constitute life. At any rate, it was Turgenev who had conceived the most striking examples of novelistic themes which took their starting point in the motive springs of character.

What James never makes fully explicit is the extent to which his gauge of fictional life relies upon a sense of human character that is remarkably consistent. The terms of James's fictional preference—a moral focus, an awareness of psychic censors, a comprehensive reflection of volitional paradoxes—imply an experiential rather than a purely sensory definition of realism. They imply that fictional life is most real, most felt, when the tensions of a psychic shift are being reenacted. Literary fables that would illuminate life must capture the interior drama of passional and prudential impulses struggling to shape experience into a liveable, meaningful configuration. Implicit in James's high evaluation of Turgenev is a bias insisting that literary realism must include the *normative* component of perception. No initiation fable could be true to life unless it reflected the felt psychic concern to redeem something of value from the exposure recently undergone. For the young James there was an exemplary truth and no small consolation in the fact that "if M. Turgénieff pays his tribute to the magic of sense he leaves us also eloquently reminded that the soul in the long run claims her own." (241) It is precisely this kind of formulation that encourages one to stress the cultural conditioning that surely informed the aesthetic sympathy between James and Turgenev. Both were "passionate pilgrims" to an internalized Mecca of civilized consciousness.

By virtue of his "presentational" rendition of life Ivan Turgenev surely qualified as one of James's most valued realists. The Russian did uphold an "ideal of delicacy" in depicting the complex motive springs of his significant fictional incidents. But the early James who enthusiastically endorsed the quality of life in Turgenev was also inclined to shrink squeamishly from Turgenev's "feel" for life. Young Henry James was more a blue-eyed American antinomian than is generally suspected. In fact, his accents could sound remarkably like those of a much later, perhaps too-often-quoted Howells: "We hold to the good old belief that the presumption, in life, is in favor of the brighter side, and we deem it, in art, an indispensable condition of our interest in a depressed observer that he should at least have tried his best to be cheerful." (249-50) From the concluding pages of James's first appraisal of Turgenev it is obvious that the Russian did not always try quite hard enough. The American was not kept suitably buoyant.

Accusations of "wanton melancholy," "abuse of irony," and "promiscuous misery" cast a pall over the generally congratulatory atmosphere of the essay. Yet James is not at all conclusive in his rhetorical exorcism of Turgenev's melancholy spirits. He is clearly disturbed by Turgenev's resigned acceptance of the dominant role of contingency over will in deciding the shape of fate. James clearly would prefer, like his famous later heroine, to affront one's destiny. Yet Turgenev's disabused approach to life-expectations has obviously made some inroads into James's faith in the efficacy of initiative. We find James seeking to formulate a revised, palatable version of a Turgenevan moral, "that there is no effective plotting for happiness, that we must take what we can get, that adversity is a capable mill-stream, and that our ingenuity must go toward making it grind our corn." (229) Ultimately, James's argument negotiates its way to a compromise phrasing that goes very far to meet Turgenev's "morbidly serious" temperament. The young American tries to make the very best out of minimal consolations: "We can welcome experience as it comes, and give it what it demands . . . so long as it contributes to swell the volume of consciousness." (251)

Rather surprisingly, it was Henry James, Sr., the philosopher-father of the artist son, who at first outstripped his namesake in penetration of and enthusiasm for Turgenev's cast of mind. As if in direct response to the 1874 essay, the elder James dispatched a personal letter to Turgenev in which he praised the Russian for a maturity not evident in British fiction, which tended either to celebrate the conquering human will or to damn the palsying effect of social convention.[13]

> You as a general thing strike a far deeper chord in the consciousness of your reader. You sink your shaft sheer through the world of outward circumstance, and of social convention, and show us ourselves in the fixed grasp of fate, so to speak, or struggling vainly to break the bonds of temperament. Superficial critics revolt at this tragic spectacle, and pronounce you cynical. They mistake the profound spirituality of your method, and do not see that what touches the earnest heart of man, and fills it with divinest love and pity for its fellow-man, is infinitely more educative than anything addressed to his frivolous and self-righteous head.

It would take nearly two years before the father's sober appreciation for Turgenev's wistful accommodation to experience struck a wholly sympathetic response in his family.

In 1876 Henry James staged a confrontation that finally pitted together the rival claims of the two novelists who, in his estimation, solicited life on more sides than any of their competitors. He confronted George Eliot and Ivan Turgenev. The occasion was a review of the recent *Daniel Deronda*; it was taken as an excuse for "A Conversation." The scenario presents a triangular debate in which two passionate and pretty parties vie for the intellectual allegiance of a judicious moderate. All their verbal posturings and poutings go for naught. These rival contenders nicely symbolize the battle for contemporary American taste between the Anglo-Saxon and the Continental factions. Pulcheria, as her name suggests, cultivates her own and other beautiful forms. She finds her literary satisfactions in French novels. Theodora, not surprisingly, appreciates the divine gift of inspiration when it is offered at the proper moral altitude. She is content to live in George Eliot's "complete world." It is Constantius, a bulwarklike gentleman, possessor of both good morals and good taste, who somewhat magisterially mediates the conversation. With his modest repute as a literary reviewer and a one-book author, Constantius speaks both authoritatively and transparently for Henry James himself. It is, therefore, to be heeded when Constantius, in his search for a balanced verdict on the battle of tastes, abruptly announces a preference: "Turgénieff is my man."[14]

That Henry James should in time discover his aesthetic and moral sensibilities best recapitulated in Turgenev was hardly an unexpected result. For, although he was upset by the implicit philosophy of life lurking between the lines in the Russian's novels, James also maintained a quarrel of longer standing over the outlook on life overtly present in George Eliot. In his first signed critical review James was already taking Eliot to task, however deferentially, for her representation and her presentation of life. "Conscience, in the classes from which George Eliot recruits her figures, is a universal gift ... the world which sums up the common traits of our author's various groups is the word *respectable* ... in each of them passion proves itself feebler than conscience."[15] The very young James, straining against the "protectionist" confines of Anglo-American moralism, dared fault even the worldly George Eliot for purveying "an atmosphere too redolent of peace and abundance" in which the only imaginable gross misery had to be a direct result of the sufferer's folly. In short, James is burdening George Eliot in 1866 with the same charge that later, for different reasons, he will level against the French realists—a lack of moral imagination. In Eliot, conventional moralism paradoxically depresses

31

the prospects for a morally interesting subject; all too frequently an Eliot novel compromises with the old tradition that "a serious story of manners shall close with the factitious happiness of a fairy tale."[16] Of course Eliot improved, and so did James's estimate of her. But even in his generally laudatory review of *Middlemarch* he finds the narrative presence of so much philosophic brain "too copious a dose" for the proper pacing and pictorial rendering of fictionalized life. "If we write novels so, how shall we write History?"[17] James's critical stance toward Eliot's greatest fictions—that in them philosophy impinged upon and violated the precincts of art—allied him with the new American orthodoxy of "dramatic method."[18] The intimidating weight of Eliot's achievement could only be shrugged off with the assistance of a Continental aesthetic. Eliot's reputation as an artist suffered irreparable damage from James's exposure to a frowning critic like Edmond Scherer.[19] It was this damage, coupled with his discontents over Eliot's world-view, that finally biased the outcome of his conversation on *Deronda*.

What is perhaps most unexpected in this staged conversation is James's willing transfer of his own aesthetic "line" to the intemperate tongue of Pulcheria. She gives a peppery enumeration of James's counts against the "diffuse" Eliot narratives, and then summarily executes the verdict—"protracted, pretentious, pedantic." Oddly, Constantius offers no resistance to the substance of this onslaught. In fact, his sole response is merely to tone down the decibel level of the attack. In venturing to be more polite, Constantius intimates a trace of condescension. "Turgénieff is a magician, which I don't think I should call George Eliot. One is a poet, the other is a philosopher. One cares for the aspect of things and the other cares for the reason of things . . . Instead of feeling life itself, it is 'views' upon life that she tries to feel."[20] As for these "views," Constantius sometimes derives a cavalier delight from Eliot's "feminine sense of consequence," especially in *Middlemarch*. "If Dorothea had married anyone after her misadventure with Casaubon, she would have married a trooper."

Still, Constantius does join Theodora's defense of Eliot at one point in the conversation. Significantly, it occurs over a thematic issue, the passionate defense of a *donnée*. When Pulcheria challenges the verisimilitude of investing frivolous Gwendolyn with an emergent tragic consciousness, Constantius immediately insists that this particular portrayal from *Deronda* is the most *intelligent* thing in all Eliot. Despite her want of artistic tact and her smuggling of ponderous philosophical cargo into the reader's range of vision, James clearly treasures the thematic sophistication Eliot has brought to a once shallow mimetic tradition. In James's defense of Gwendolyn's story, there is a commitment to give literary realism more depth by mediating reality through an experiential focus. In James's definition of Gwendolyn's drama, there is a sweeping recognition of the role of contingency in human affairs. "The universe forcing itself with a slow, inexorable pressure into a narrow, complacent, and yet after all extremely sensitive mind, and making it ache with the pain of the process."[21] Precisely this theme, the expense of an expanded awareness, is as much typical of Turgenev as of Eliot. By 1876 Henry James had surely reached full awareness of the aesthetic, perceptual, and even thematic sympathies that bound him closer and closer to the orbit of Ivan Turgenev.

What had happened in so brief an interval to cause James to install Turgenev as titular head of his novelistic pantheon? In the letters of William James in 1876 to his brother in Paris we can eavesdrop on the shift of conviction that converted the James sons to their father's way of thinking.[22]

> I never heard you speak so enthusiastically of any human being ...
> although the vein of 'morbidness' was so pronounced in the stories,
> yet the mysterious depths which his plummet sounds atone for all. It
> is the amount of life which a man feels that makes you value his
> mind, and Turguénieff has a sense of worlds within worlds whose
> existence is unsuspected by the vulgar, [whereas] ... [Eliot's]
> 'sapience', as you excellently call it, passes all decent bounds. There
> is something essentially womanish in the irrepressible garrulity of her
> moral reflections ... hence the tedious iteration and restlessness of
> George Eliot's commentary on life.

It was, apparently, a case of familiarity with Turgenev breeding fondness. Ten days after his arrival in Paris in November 1875, Henry James gained entrée at No. 50 Rue de Douai—and there is good reason to believe that the resident there was the main attraction in the city for the well-traveled and well-lettered young American.[23]

Much of Henry James's "Paris year" of apprenticeship (November 1875 to September 1876) remains hidden in obscurity or cloaked in perhaps deliberate confusion. We know that what James desired "more than anything else" in the summer of 1874 before he was summoned home on "practical grounds" was "a *régal* of intelligent and suggestive society, especially male"; entry into such a group, whether in Paris or

33

London, would, he was sure, increase his powers of application.[24] What unlimited enthusiasm, then, one might expect when that "most approachable genius," Turgenev, regularly ushered the young American into the famous Flaubert *cénacle* of intelligent, suggestive male company! And yet James rather effectively publicized among American contemporaries the extent to which he found defective the "wares [of] the little rabble of Flaubert's satellites." By July he announced to his brother, with a surprising lack of moderation, the falling away of his "last layers of resistance to a long-encroaching weariness and satiety with the French mind." "I have done with 'em, forever, and am turning English all over."[25] In capsule, the story that most of James's letters tell about his first-hand introduction to the French realists is a dramatic progression from aloof interest to disaffection to denunciation. But the full story, as one would expect of a champion of consciousness, is much more ambivalent.

Leon Edel has wisely cautioned us to make generous allowance for the circumstantiality of these intemperate utterances.[26] And judging from a letter to John Hay, Howells himself would have been very startled to hear that his friend had embraced an ethnocentric perspective on things. "Henry James is gone abroad not to return, I fancy, even for visits."[27] For the unpublicized version of the Parisian apprenticeship, one should scan James's letters to T. S. Perry. It is in addressing this fellow connoisseur of Continental delicacies that James releases his exuberance (in French!) over having found at last a literary company worth keeping. *"Tu vois que je suis dans les conceils des dieux—que je suis lancé en plein olympe."*[28] In converse with Perry, James reveals a rather more frequent and intimate relationship with his French peers than he admits elsewhere. Reverently agog before the twin colossi of Paris, Turgenev and Flaubert, and suitably discriminating about the limitations of the satellite talents, we see a Henry James whose moral sensitivities can withstand considerable stretching in the name of art. It takes a Zola to break that tolerance. As late as June 1876, *after* Turgenev's departure for Russia, a cheerfully creative James can report to Perry, "I am decently busy, & more & more Parisian."[29]

It is certainly possible to imagine a milder termination of the "Paris year" than the bearish bolt for London related to brother William, whom Henry enjoyed teasing for his excessive moral reactions when abroad. Perhaps James had simply extracted his fill of experience. After completing on location his novel, *The American*, and after curtailing his onerous but remunerative *Tribune* letters, James matter-of-factly discovered "there is nothing else, for me personally, on the horizon and it is rather ignoble to stay in Paris simply for the restaurants."[30]

Despite the two contradictory versions of the visits *chez Flaubert*, not all the emotional traces of the American in Paris in 1876 were blurred by James's own ambivalent testimony. It remains clear that 1876 was a *Lehrjahr* and that much of the learning done that year was assimilated from Turgenev. Some of the learning was, of course, technical—related to the craft of evoking the illusion of verisimilitude.[31] In fact, James's most exuberant letter to Perry was sparked by a two-hour discourse in which Turgenev detailed the procedures of conceptualization and craftsmanship that produced an archetypal Bazarov out of a pallid real-life model. The young American was both flattered and reassured to find that the "first novelist of the day" upheld in person the character-centered novel and the methods of characterology which had been ascribed to him. But even more important than selected doctrines of the writing craft was another sort of learning.

From James's letters we can watch him absorbing from Turgenev a well-balanced posture of hospitality toward the multiple forms that cultures observe. James was emulating a wise and worldly provincial. The Parisian Russians in general set an instructive precedent for him. They are, he wrote his father, "quite the most (to me) fascinating people one can see; with their personal ease and *désinvolture* and that atmosphere of general culture and curiosity which they owe to having (through their possession of many languages) windows open all round the horizon."[32] Turgenev in particular combined a perfectly natural air of insouciance with a solid foundation in moral depths—a combination that both unnerved and enticed the as yet vicarious aesthete from America. The spectacle of the revered Russian "at his age and with his glories" contorting himself in charades struck James as a wondrous example of the European spontaneity sadly inaccessible to American men of substance. Turgenev's whole life style posed a challenge to the ingrained American suspicion that the art of sociability requires a behavioral agility that precludes the retention of ethical principle. The cosmopolite Russian had first to be recognized as a phenomenon before he could serve as a model for conscious emulation. In one of James's more vitriolic letters about the Paris literary scene, this recognition of the extraordinary is registered. The Russian author, *in propria persona*, is found to be "morally interesting." His presence and demeanor amidst the French school added a needed elasticity to the American James's moral imagination. "Turgenev is worth the whole heap of them, and yet he himself swallows them down in a manner that excites my extreme wonder. . . . He is so pure and strong a genius that he doesn't need to be on the defensive as regards his opinions and enjoyments."[33] Clearly, the "wares" Turgenev offered, unlike the more publicized French commodities, were as if designed to meet the American's specifications for a decently broad life-horizon. The Russian's carriage opened up a path to safe conduct, one that permitted a maximum exposure to the hazards of experience without risking the sacrifice of a felt need for moral composure.

A clear confirmation of the centrality of extraliterary factors in welding the firm aesthetic ties between James and Turgenev rises out of the moving memorial essay of 1884.[34] For so extensive a tribute, surprisingly little is said of Turgenev's much-heralded "dramatic method." But a great deal is revealed about the cultural and attitudinal affinities that lured the young American to recognize in the elderly Russian "a singularly complete human being." (294) First, there is a joyous pronouncement of the emancipatory effect this one artist had on a nervous Victorian consciousness. "He felt and understood the opposite sides of life; he was imaginative, speculative, anything but literal . . . Our Anglo-Saxon, Protestant, moralistic, conventional standards were far away from him, and he judged things with a freedom and spontaneity in which I found a perpetual refreshment." (296) Second, and equally important, there was in this Russian a reassuring capacity for crucial restraints and renunciations. "Cosmopolite that he had become by the force of circumstances, his roots had never been loosened in native soil." (292) And the secret sustenance he derived from "the great back-garden of his Slav imagination" fortified him in rebutting the "new votaries of realism." "It was this air that he carried about with him of feeling all the variety of life, of knowing strange and far-off things, of having an horizon in which the Paris horizon—so familiar, so wanting in mystery, so perpetually *exploité*—easily lost itself, that distinguished him from these companions." (304) Recognizing Turgenev's decorousness and discrimination, James reserves the fullest measure of his gratitude for Turgenev's role as a liberator. In the valedictory essay to Turgenev there is a nearly rapturous recognition of a blessed precedent having been set. In Turgenev, the decent American famished for experience and exposure had the example of a moral imagination uninhibited by moralizing. The Russian had the grace of right perception; he could assimilate Flaubert's methods (and even

Zola's observations) into a higher poetry of life. It is a fine insight of James's that the quality of Turgenev's imagination, not his narrative methods, could most teach Americans how to entertain and be entertained by the often melancholy play of human inspiration against external contingencies and random events. Thus, even while bidding farewell to Turgenev, James can greet the newly-expanded future of a viable postbellum American realism.

> It is not open to us as yet to discuss whether a novel had better be an excision from life or a structure built up of picture-cards, for we have not made up our mind as to whether life in general may be described . . . But individuals may feel their way, and perhaps even pass unchallenged, if they remark that for them the manner in which Turgénieff worked will always seem the most fruitful. (316)

Upon receipt of the news of Turgenev's death in September 1883, Henry James wrote the editor of *Atlantic*: "I am greatly touched by his extinction—I wanted him to live—mainly, I am afraid, because I wanted to see him again; *for he had done his work.*"[35] A month before, James had contributed an essay to *Century Magazine* that proclaimed, "the French may bear the palm today in the representation of manners by the aid of fiction," and that in particular "Alphonse Daudet is at the head of his profession."[36] Even James's memorial essay to Turgenev can be seen, with much justice, to signal a precocious, if cautious, American defense of French naturalism.[37] And it is now known that James, in February 1884, actively solicited an intermediary to reestablish contacts and provide for reentry into the same Parisian fraternity for which he had once affected distaste.[38] All these signs would seem to indicate that James had outgrown, or defected from, Turgenev's "middle path" at a rapid pace. But even the clearest signs can be misread in haste.

Given his age and physical condition, Turgenev could not long serve as a current exemplar of the literary values the young James wished to see perpetuated. Also, the Russian's long-awaited *Virgin Soil* (1877) did indisputably disappoint even his most avid American cultists. The elderly novelist had allegedly indulged an old man's prerogative—that of taking the present to task—to the detriment of his famed art of impartial narrative. Yet Henry James was rather less discouraged than most American reviewers. Perhaps because he was less addicted to invoking the new orthodoxy of "dramatic method," James found it easier to acknowledge substantial merits. "Turgenef always shows his superiority in the choice of his subjects; his themes are never conventional and stale; he is certain to select a *donnée* which means and reveals something."[39] In short, James continued to extract suggestive mental ore from Turgenev's underlying thematic and situational probes. But rather soon after James came to know the "beautiful genius," Turgenev's novel-sized inventiveness began to flag. The result in James was a perceptible shift of emulative sight onto the lively aesthetic experiments of the budding French "Naturalists." If anything, though, the sensibility of Turgenev was honored rather than violated in James's transfer of focus.

The remarkable essay on Daudet sets about distinguishing the Provençal (hence, provincial) genius from his Parisian colleagues. The distinguishing marks selected have a familiar look about them. We are told that Daudet lacks "the hardness of consistent realism" and that, unlike his rivals, his imagination displays a salutary "horror of the literal, the limited; it sees an object in all its intermingled relations—on its sentimental, its pathetic, its comical, its pictorial side." (501) In other words, Daudet is being advanced for qualities that make him a substitute Turgenev; he, too, partakes of the Turgenevan insight that *perception, "realistically" apprehended, is a value-creating event.* It is characteristic of James's essential loyalty to Turgenev that he defends French Naturalism insofar as "it has opened its eyes well to the fact that the magic of the arts of representation lies in their appeal to the associations awakened by things." (501) This is tantamount to saying, "No realism without the stressed presence of a mediating consciousness." The master's voice can be heard posthumously in a stern warning James issued to Daudet after he had indulged in externalized characterization. "Il n'y a rien de plus réel, de plus positif, de plus à peindre, qu'un charactère; c'est là qu'on trouve bien la couleur et la forme."[40] Henry James's new-found openness to French visions of reality was very much accomplished on Turgenev's terms of accommodation.

Morris Roberts has categorized the decade from 1873 to 1883 as the period of James's "real apprenticeship," a period that conveniently and, I believe, significantly coincides with James's heightened awareness of Ivan Turgenev.[41] Roberts further locates the first sign of transition from the early to the mature James in his 1880 reevaluation of Sainte-Beuve. "He has discovered that morality in a writer does not consist in laying down formal precepts, that thought is not confined to the formulation of general principles, that there is both thought and morality in what he calls the importing of life into literature."[42] It would be my contention that the discoveries James made about the foreclosed opportunities that were the cost of prescriptive criticism, the discoveries so eloquently announced in the *donnée*-granting liberality of his "The Art of Fiction," were discoveries prompted by his close association since 1876 with the wide Slavic nature of Ivan Turgenev. The Henry James of 1884 who so boldly proclaimed his capacity to entertain dispassionately "a myriad forms" of humanly-refracted reality had re-created himself largely in the image of the Russian cosmopolite. The uprooted Russian guided the peripatetic American to the mind-expanding perception that reality was not all realism, a codified attitude, but simply the total variety of phenomenological experience. It was through Turgenev that the serious study of art became "a revelation of freedom" for James as critic. "There is no impression of life, no manner of seeing it and feeling it, to which the plan of the novelist may not offer a place."[43]

What remains to be shown is that the vision of life "imported" into literature by the early James as artist largely coincided with the implicit world-view in Turgenev's fiction. By 1884 Henry James knew enough what he was about to correct an admiring female novelist's rendering of life.[44]

Morality is hot—but art is icy! . . . *life* is less criminal, less obnoxious, less objectionable, less crude, more *bon enfant*, more mixed and casual, *and even in its most offensive manifestations*, more *pardonable*, than the unholy circle with which you have surrounded your heroine.

Now, the tendency here evident—the Olympian disposition to grant clemency to life's overall conduct, the faith in the possibility of retrieving value out of the harshest experience—is a tendency equally prominent in Turgenev's fully articulated versions of life. What remained for the mature Henry James, above and beyond perceiving Turgenev's redemptive aesthetic, his clement vision, was to replicate that consciousness in a kindred yet idiosyncratic style. One thing was certain. The magic behind Turgenev's transfigurative performance, even in translation, was stylistic. With the sure touch of a connoisseur, James singled out in Turgenev "the beauty of the finest presentation of the familiar ... the effect, for the commonest truth, of an exquisite envelope of poetry."[45] And, having absorbed the lesson of *this* master, James did go on to demonstrate that he, too, could allow the aesthetic sense full play without violating inner decency; that he, too, could write prose poems of reconciliation to the antipoetic compromises of mundane living. For, unlike Robert Frost's "Oven Bird," whose mournful plaint of disenchantment enervates the listener, Turgenev and James both knew, when sore pressed, "what to make of a diminished thing."

CHAPTER FOUR

Tales of Initiation (1874-79)

In the Roman spring of 1873 Henry James was discomforted by his rather narrow repute as a reviewer and critic. Exasperated, he finally disclosed his secret ambitions to Grace Norton, his most-favored confidante. "To produce some little exemplary works of art is my narrow and lowly dream. They are to have less 'brain' than *Middlemarch*, but (I boldly proclaim it) they are to have more *form*."[1] The bold aspirant rapidly proved good on his promise. That very summer, in Bad Homburg, Henry James wrote *Madame de Mauves* and conceived "Eugene Pickering," both of which may be regarded as pivotal tales. They mark James's turn toward the "international theme," in which involuntary cosmopolitan amours serve to objectify a psychic tug of war between strained cultural loyalties.[2] That same summer James was rereading Turgenev's works in preparation for his *North American Review* essay. Even after completing his exhaustive critique, James did not act as if he had "done" Turgenev. The following summer he chose Baden-Baden as his work retreat, hoping to encounter Turgenev or at least to soak up some residuary inspiration from the surroundings, for, as he explained to his father, "many of his tales were probably written here—which proves that the place is favorable to literary labor."[3] As fate would have it, James neither met Turgenev nor worked well in Baden-Baden. But his ardor for the Russian master was not dampened by these reverses. In fact, he brought a missionary zeal back from Europe in the late autumn of 1874.

Still extant from that period is a brief note from the young James to the venerable Longfellow recommending Turgenev's tales as "the best short stories ever written—to my knowledge."[4] Such a superlative estimate of Turgenev's short fiction was not a passing fancy. In the summer of 1878 in response to a request from W. E. Henley for bibliographical guidance, James confessed that he liked "the idea of helping any one, in any degree" to read Turgenev, and even envied any one "the high pleasure of making acquaintance with him." Then, as if to prove the extent of his own devotion, James recalled (with his own Turgenev collection an ocean away) a comparative bibliography of translations which included "in back volumes of the *Revue des Deux Mondes* 10 and 15 years ago—2 or 3 *superb* things of T's."[5] That Henry James, particularly in the 1870s, possessed an intimate knowledge, even an expertise, in the fiction of Ivan Turgenev cannot be gainsaid.

Yet despite James's demonstrable intimacy with the works of Turgenev, it is a delicate task to convert such certain knowledge into proof of influence. Indeed, a lot of knowledge can be a dangerous temptation in a comparativist investigation. One can be so certain, given the overwhelming evidence of an impact, that telltale traces of influence *must* exist in the texts that gross similarities get violently yoked together to fasten an argument.[6] There can be a mindless literalism about specific textual details that proves more about the investigator's avidity than anything about an organic, genetic relationship between texts. But there is also an antithetical danger. It is possible to conduct a discussion of influence on such a level of generality that the particular juxtaposition being advanced becomes empirically undemonstrable or, quite simply, beside the point. Discussions of narrative technique in the abstract can easily wrap a tenebrous haze around an influence study. While it is important to recognize, as Edna Kenton has, that James until around 1876 was an experimental teller of tales, trying out technical variants of first-person narrative, the source of any particular variant is usually untraceable and, in any case, insignificant *as such*.[7] James very early found it effective to mediate a fictional incident through the eye-lens of a passive witness, allowing the story to be viewed, as outside events are in life, from a "wandering periphery."[8] But how do we locate the narrative prototype, say, of the 1867 tale, "My Friend Bingham"? The device of the norm-setting friend-narrator could have derived with equal ease from Turgenev ("My Neighbor Radilov") or from Mérimée. Mere temporal priority in a single structural detail, wholly divorced from the semantic matrix of the achieved narrative, is barren of significance. How, then, can one *legitimately* speak of a literary influence as *seminal*? A persuasive argument must enlist our belief in, and enrich our comprehension of, the inspirational shock of recognition sparked between two creative artists.

As for establishing legitimacy, James scholarship has been fortunate in being able to build upon the solid intelligence of Cornelia Pulsifer Kelley's pioneering influence study. She bequeathed to future critics a well-documented definition of how the early James's imagination submitted itself to influences. Far more important than a static catalogue of borrowed materials, Kelley gave us a conceptual model of the morphology of a Jamesian apprenticeship tale. Applying her careful scholarship to the James tales of the 1870s, she demonstrated that James typically composed "morally interesting" fictional "cases" by entertaining variations on his travel and reading experiences.[9]

> James allowed Balzac, Mérimée, Musset, to give him not just suggestions for method or manner of writing but the germs of his stories. He saw possibilities which these authors had not developed or made the most of—other ways of treating similar situations, or the reverse situation—and proceeded to develop a story on his own initiative. It cannot be said that he plagiarized ... in taking hints from other authors, in reversing their situations, he was merely doing what he had already done as regards his own stories.

In short, Kelley has shown us that profound influences on the early James are most apt to be detected by situational analysis. James did not borrow stylistic mannerisms or isolated plot constituents. He recogitated fundamental predicaments already bodied forth in particular fictional actions. Therefore, a significant influence on James would work on his imagination at the level of the *basic fable* underlying the realized plot.[10] In this chapter, my constant effort will be to "eavesdrop" as James manipulates variations on particular rites of passage previously imagined by Turgenev.

As a preliminary step to a clearer overlook, it may be helpful to get some notion as to which sorts of Turgenev tales most intrigued or excited Henry James in the 1870s. If we look closely at James's comprehensive critique of 1874, we shall find amidst the many stories momentarily admired, a few that are more evidently treasured. Most notably, "to a person able to read but one of M. Turgénieff's tales," James would offer as a supreme example of analysis elevated to artistry "The Brigadier."[11] What makes this story so admirable to James is that it manages not to be lachrymose while dealing with a hero made

43

imbecilic by suffering. Romance, James says, has extracted a credible fragrance out of a case of moral decomposition. Keeping this in mind, we should note that in his letter to Henley, James singled out "Living Relics" as a small masterpiece.[12] Here again we have a case of a person in a state of extreme decomposition successfully managing to aestheticize, even to beatify all experience. As we shall observe later, "First Love," another influential Turgenev tale, also converts a humiliating existence into poeticized perception. We can say, then, that James very early maintained an unqualified admiration for those tales of Turgenev that depicted (usually indirectly) states of consciousness in the process of transforming the anti-poetic dross of life into an epiphanic vision. Yet however much James admired the artistry of such tales, he admits that their substance remained remote from his experience. All too often the Turgenevan epiphanic tale stressed the self-redemptive visionary powers of mental invalids—simpletons and fanatics; hence, even moments of beatitude were cast over with melancholy and pathos. But there was a species of Turgenevan short fiction that dealt with levels of consciousness less remote from James. These were the quotidian tales about waste, lost fulfillment, and resignation.

The single tale mentioned in more places and arousing more agitation than any other in the 1874 essay is "A Correspondence." It is over this "polished piece of misery" that James most agonizes; for Turgenev's very capacity to conceive such a dismal outcome suspends an alienating "dusky pall of fatality . . . over all human things" and reduces the human will to an empty parody of real achievement.[13] The outcome in question involves the sudden eruption of an enslaving libido, sundering forever what had been the slowly converging natural affinity between a high-minded intellectual and a charming, honest "philosophess." It is not the sadness of this sundering that depresses James; it is the will-lessness of the sufferers that is saddening.

James was strongly attracted to the Turgenev who had moral imagination enough to see the eloquence latent in "a pair of lovers accepting adversity." Life in Turgenev not only included the ascetic impulse, it could even be enriched by renunciation. The Turgenev James was willing to emulate conceived recurring designs "to paint the natural conflict between soul and sense." James perceived an archetypal predicament, a basic fable, in Turgenev that was prior to any particular thematic elaboration; it postulated situations that exposed an internal tension, an ambivalent attraction, involving the rival domains of "sense" and "soul." Given such situations, James clearly thought the contest should be nearly, but not quite, even. "If M. Turgénieff pays his tribute to the magic of sense he leaves us also eloquently reminded that soul in the long run claims her own."

Unfortunately, the terms of this fundamental polarity, "soul" versus "sense," do not translate easily into the more circumscribed, precisely-defined "tensions" that one expects to be detailed by a modern close reader. The particular and intimate dilemma which surely informs James's genteel, abstract diction is not easily unveiled. The language is carefully circumspect, but James persistently implies that life, as he understands it, gradually impales a growing consciousness on the sharp antagonism between ethical and aesthetic impulses. And Turgenev, at his best, depicts either the melancholy spectacle of a permanent and involuntary impasse, or, occasionally, the heroic attainment of intensest beauty through following the paradoxical path of a voluntary asceticism. This latter possibility, that of the higher consciousness of the conscientious, the superior delectations vouchsafed to the dutiful, struck James as being very American. James could easily admire and believe in the fulfillments enjoyed by Turgenev's maiden visionaries. "It is the women and young girls in our author's tales who mainly represent strength of will—the power to resist, to wait, to attain."[14] Turgenev had in fact anticipated James's own celebration of the moral spontaneity of provincial girlhood, his canonization of spontaneous ascetics.

Therefore one can begin to appreciate James's feeling of upset, almost betrayal, over "A Correspondence." Rightly or wrongly, James felt that Turgenev was, for once, jilting the naturally austere type, cruelly depriving her of a heroine's *willed* renunciation; here Turgenev seemed to be embittered, sardonically affirming "the fatal victory of sense." In and by itself, this brief cruel tale could perhaps have been dismissed. But, by 1873, Henry James was seriously wondering why it should seem "a matter of course for the author that base passion should carry the day." The pattern of "A Correspondence" was recurring. And James was getting concerned enough to initiate his first variation on a Turgenev situation.

So panoramic was James's 1874 essay on Turgenev that it is easy to pass over his reference to the occasion which stimulated it. The pretext for James's extensive article was a single text under review, the recent *Spring Torrents* (1871).[15] Turgenev's latest work, as James rightly saw, was a reworking of earlier plot structures. Only four years previously, the novel *Smoke* had also depicted the defection of a romantic lover to the rank company of victims seduced by a debasing passion. Lest

James's concern appear exaggerated, it should be mentioned that associates very close to Turgenev found his latest repetitious dénouement controversial, even sinister.[16] Even Turgenev's most intimate Russian literary adviser failed to understand a protagonist "capable of smacking his lips over the bouquet of divine ambrosia and of tearing at raw meat like a Kalmyk, all with the same relish."[17] Oddly enough, some American responses were among the most sympathetic; Howells, for instance, found it Turgenev's "greatest book," praising its naked and unsparing portrayal of "the terribleness of a guilty passion."[18]

Henry James, too, however depressing he found the subject, was willing to concede the "wonderful mysteries" of the "swarming, shifting possibilities" of youth's spring-time torrents. His acceptance of the *donnée*, one suspects, is aided by the fact that the catastrophic love is recollected in the actively penitential mind of the protagonist. Hence the whole sad history, for James, can be weighted "with the moral that salvation lies in being able, at a given moment, to turn on one's will like a screw." In contrast to "A Correspondence" James could claim that the casualties idealistic romance sustained in *Spring Torrents* did not necessarily imply any fatal victory for sensualism. The morbid imagination behind the *donnée* was redeemed by the elegiac tone of the narrative. Clearly, James read the story as a cautionary tale.

In fact, Turgenev's *Veshnie Vody* (in the original) is both more profound and more disturbing than James's remarks would indicate.[19] That James suspected the protagonist's fall might be ambiguous is suggested by his keen perception that the uncorrupted female in the tale is only a "half-sister" to other Turgenev heroines; she displays a banal taste for popular comedy and vulgar mimicry. James may have sensed that she was a bit too theatrical to be a quite solid prop against seduction. In many subtle ways Turgenev's narrative conspires to question the genuine value of the tale's "light" (but not fair) heroine, the somewhat precious Gemma. On the other hand, the narrative is unambivalently about the irresistible claim of the authentic chthonian powers as they are voluptuously embodied in the "dark" (but fair-complexioned) heroine, Madame Polozova. *Veshnie Vody* tells of a harsh initiation into loveless sexuality, but the initiation is a mixed blessing in disguise. The story is related in a manner perfectly suited for a subtle signaling to the reader. It is an omniscient impersonal narrative that purports to reconstruct a thirty-year-old catastrophe as recalled by a now-penitent Russian of fifty-two with a serious case of *Weltschmerz*. This mode of narration permits a double perspective: the reminiscences of Dmitri Pavlovich Sanin are constantly being commented upon by an unobtrusive authorial presence. These ironic Turgenevan innuendoes transform the oldest story in the world, an amorous triangle, into a multi-layered symbolic action.

The greater part of the story reconstructs the precarious idyll of an ingenuous traveling Russian nobleman with a seller of Italian confectionary, Gemma Roselli. Henry James was quite correct to emphasize how "very young" and "very Russian" the protagonist is; Sanin's imagination concocts a sentimental dalliance, exactly the sort of cosmopolitan pastiche to enchant a Russian Romantic of the 1840s. The exceptionality, the sheer freakishness of this romance makes it the stuff of parody. A Russian serf-owner exchanges compliments in French with an Italian republican in the temporarily "free city" of Frankfurt, Germany. Sanin's love is accelerated by an atmosphere of charming fraud. The couple see each other in stereotypical images drawn from second-rate art; the would-be mother-in-law delights in finding some very dubious similitudes in the sounds of Italian and Russian; Sanin wins precedence in Gemma's heart by engaging in the by then farcical and undangerous convention of dueling. The likelihood of a grand passion developing out of a domestic environment that contains stock characters from the *commedia dell'arte* is remote. As if for confirmation of this point we are given a scene in which Gemma reads from Malz's German imitations of bourgeois comedy. "By what miracle," Sanin wonders, "could such an ideally beautiful face take on suddenly such comic and sometimes even banal expressions." But it is no wonder, considering that we are told "love scenes especially were unsuited to her." (41) The pathos of this false idyll is only fully revealed when serious attempts are made to make it real. The financial arrangements essential to sustain a lasting union require Sanin to contemplate selling humans as chattel. In its attempted realization the innocent republican romance is first compromised, then undermined. The cosmopolitan, democratic union cannot subsist without some substantial backing; for that, Frankfurt must negotiate with Weisbaden, Sanin must come to terms with all that Polozova represents. The deepest symbolic action in *Veshnie Vody* sadly underscores the pathetic career of Romantic politics, philosophy, and psychology: a fabric composed whole cloth of spun-together allusions must fade and tear when superimposed on rough, inchoate "life."[20]

Polozova is a creature of awesome symbolic dimensions. In gauging her full stature, no detail can be overlooked. Etymologically her conjugal name includes the suggestion of sex *(pol)* as well as a specific reference to the runner *(poloz)* of a sleigh *(sani)*, a sinister hidden clue to her easy guidance of Sanin. But by no means is all her suggestiveness covert. Consider the overt irony in Turgenev's rendition of Sanin's first encounter with her. "Any man who met her would have stood stock still (and not unwillingly), not before a 'tabernacle of beauty,' to speak in Pushkin's words, but rather before the enchantment of a powerful, partly-Russian, partly-Gypsy, blooming woman's body. Yet the image of Gemma protected Sanin, like that triple armor of which poets sing." (107) Here, in capsule, we have the juxtaposition of impotent poetic formulations against a visceral, protean force. Significantly, Turgenev makes explicit efforts to give this dark force very specific associations. Polozova speaks "an amazingly pure, true Moscow Russian—the way the people, not the gentry, speak." (110) Whereas Sanin likes art and "everything beautiful," Polozova likes "only Russian songs—and then, only in the country, in the springtime, with dancing." This same Polozova "most of all could not tolerate sanctimoniousness, phrase-mongering, or lies." (121) It is with "undoubted sincerity and sobriety" that she confesses her greatest love is for freedom; having since childhood seen her fill of serfdom and having lost patience with it, she has deliberately married herself to an indolent sluggard who is content to watch in apathy his "free Cossack." (125) Sanin's fatal woman is laden with seductive cultural associations. Polozova embodies the full pagan allure of an anarchic and atavistic *folk* Russia. And despite his high culture and sentimental ideals, part of Sanin is enslaved by this rude vitalistic beauty. Sanin, of course, regrets it—he still yearns for the milder, decorous contours of Gemma. But Turgenev refuses to imply that Sanin's catastrophic initiation, though costly and pathetic, was of no redeeming social importance. In the end Gemma is released from her ties to an inhospitable central Europe; her sentimental aspirations get transplanted to a more appreciative soil as she blissfully thrives in the merchant republic of New York City. And Sanin, as is only natural, wistfully dreams of uniting someday with what America now promises. But meanwhile, when he does pursue education, he reads "not periodicals, but serious books, histories." (140) In this case, the youthful torrents of spring have been a mere prelude to an immersion in the deluge of repressed, archaic energies. Turgenev's Russians are often very cosmopolitan, but they share an indigenous nature too.

What Henry James literally "made" of *Spring Torrents* is interesting to compare with the preceding interpretation of the Russian text. We know that, in rereading Turgenev in the summer of 1873, James had become somewhat agitated over what he mistakenly interpreted as a tendency to reduce life to a series of "victories of sense over soul." In reaction, the young James deliberately set out to complicate the *donnée* by imagining an exceptional and contrary case. The model for the sort of situational reversal James affected can be seen in *Madame de Mauves*, the most famous product of that summer. The eponymous heroine of that work is, as Cornelia Kelley first deduced from the given maiden name, an Americanized version of the title figure in *La Princesse de Clèves*; this Euphemia Cleve is also, as her first name indicates, a paragon of euphemistic as well as of "precious" virtue.[21] In a similar manner, Turgenev's *Spring Torrents* is the structural archetype for James's obverse case in "Eugene Pickering" (1874). As pedantic proofs of the influence one could cite telltale details such as the fact that James's male *ingenue* is also removed to Weisbaden to execute his ambiguous fall; also exactly like Turgenev, James deliberately reverses the convention of the "dark lady" by bedecking her in "a good deal of blond hair" and in "white muslin very much puffed and frilled." (301)[22] But even more revealing than pedantic proofs are the situational parallels and twists.

"Eugene Pickering" is the story of an extreme innocent and his ingenuous temptress, *both* of whom are seduced by a world of prefabricated images. But it is a story with a happy ending, which in this case means that the excesses committed are imagined, then expelled, with the result that both parties can rise to final victories of "soul." It is a story in which the natural forces of life vanquish some maiming conventions of society and art, yet life itself remains social and decorous. It is as if the roles of Gemma and Polozova were merged, the twin dangers were surmounted, and Sanin were released to marry an authentic Turgenev heroine from another novel. James's intrigue begins to take shape amidst the "long shafts of unnatural light" that give a glittery casino excitement to the entire resort of Hamburg. Gradually we discern, through the eyes of a friend-narrator, the interesting posture of Eugene Pickering, in whom (to anticipate) "opportunity was not offering a meaning to the empty forms with which his imagination was stored." (307) All asprawl and agape, reclining in awe before the celestial strains of Weber's "Prayer" from *Die Freischutz* as accompanied by the clinking sounds of bet-making and risk-taking in the background, Pickering is the very picture of "overt wonderment." In fact, James has proposed the extreme case of experiential impoverishment: a cloistered, virginal "Juliet" to his schoolfellows, the heir and understudy of "a sort of high-priest of the proprieties," the paternally-pledged bridegroom of a similarly secluded mate, Pickering's countenance expresses "the perfection of inexperience." But he is now encountered during the first breathing spell of his virtually corseted life. In this vulnerable, anticipatory state he is beckoned to by what looks to be an experienced adventuress; he is solicited to play her gambling hunch with his uninitiated hand. The novice's embarrassed participation is James's way of foreshadowing Pickering's entrance into yet subtler games of risk. Once parsimonious, Pickering has now found a place to spend his "great accumulated fund of unuttered things of all sorts to get rid of." (323)

The repository of his emotional investment is no less fanciful a case than is Pickering himself. Madame Blumenthal immediately impresses our "impartial" narrator as "such a German, somehow, as I had seen imaged in literature . . . a friend of poets, a correspondent of philosophers, a muse, a priestess of aesthetics." (301) This valuation is later pared down to scale by a worldly Austrian diplomat-confidant who informs our witness that the adventuress is in fact a widowed bluestocking, conspicuously emancipated in her views, but most likely a *theoretic* rebel only, with an "imagination lodged where her heart should be." (328) On more direct testimony, "La Blumenthal" emerges as a passionate authoress and chamber actress whose passions are decidedly of a transcendental and sentimental stamp. She is an ingenuous siren, as is the soliloquizing Cleopatra from her "dream-play" of that name. "What, after all, is life but sensation, and sensation but deception?—reality that pales before the light of one's dreams, as Octavia's dull beauty fades before mine?" (320) This piquant mixture of nebular intellectuality and well-turned corporeal grace is admirably suited to seduce a high-minded emotional starveling like Pickering. But, vice-versa, the picturesque plight of the unemancipated American struggling to overthrow the stifling constraints of paternal honor is a scene calculated to tempt the indulgence of a Madame Blumenthal.

In brief, James's "dark lady" is no hard-hearted vamp. Much like Turgenev's Gemma, the essential unreality of her charm is exposed in her heady (or should one say hearty?) republicanism. James makes his German George Sand rabidly pro-American. "I should like to see the wonderful spectacle of a great people free to do everything it chooses, and yet never doing anything wrong!" (332) Clearly we are in gullible, not villainous, company. Both Pickering and his temptress deserve to be exculpated as "sincere attitudinizers," defined by the narrator as characters who "cultivate fictitious emotions in perfect good faith." (335) Both are enraptured by romantic conventions of each other's spiritual legacies. By chancing involvement they confront the "other" and are liberated from the intoxication of romantic clichés. After Pickering is led to commit himself to a foreign allegiance in Wiesbaden, Madame Blumenthal has no desire to take further advantage of his inexperience. She has helped him draw on his hoarded emotional capital, to indulge his reserves of sentiment. But he is not prepared for her switch to a grave, steady, non-fiction-reading Prussian major—the real man in her life. Just as she disappoints Pickering in her ultimate allegiance to a mundane respectability, he disappoints her in proving incapable of playing the "explanation scene" with a picturesque verve and outrage. They are quits, and a reconciliation with reality is engineered. Here, the passage from innocence to experience does not constitute a fall. As Pickering concedes: "It's worth it all, almost, to have been wound up for an hour to that celestial pitch." (343)

As in Turgenev's *Torrents*, except more so, the ordeal of initiation is therapeutic. Pickering, despite his initial seclusion, is American enough to espouse and act upon the principle of voluntary association. "What I claim is simply freedom to try to be!" (340) Thus, the American innocent, unlike the Russian, is not additionally humiliated by the spectacle of his own disfiguring lack of will. There are traces, though, especially in the distance between the narrator and Pickering, of a recurring undercurrent in James's work, what Stephen Spender has called "a conflict between the desire to plunge into experience, and the prudent resolution (leading eventually to a certain prudishness), to remain a spectator."[23] As Spender shapes it, this would seem to be a classic Jamesian debate over the respective merits of experience and renunciation. But even as early as "Eugene Pickering" it is a dialogue about the definition and scope of experience itself.

In an eloquent confessional sequence, James captures Pickering in the first feverish flush of his realization that he is "an active, sentient, intelligent creature" poised nervously on the brink of life's "great surging sea," "charmed by the smell of the brine and yet afraid of the water." (310) As the internal dialectic works itself out, Pickering concludes: "I honestly believe I may safely take out a license to amuse myself . . . Pleasure and pain are empty words to me; what I long for is knowledge,—some other knowledge than comes to us in formal, colorless, impersonal precept." (311) But the worldly (if not wholly reliable) narrator has an immediate rejoinder. "Your long seclusion makes you think the world better worth knowing than you're likely to find it. A man with as good a head and heart as yours *has a very ample world within himself*, and I'm no believer in art for art, nor in what's called 'life' for life's sake."[24] The question raised is whether one can best entertain the widest range of felt life through an imaginative or a participatory engagement. It is important to realize that "plunging" and "renunciation" are *both* modes of engaging experience. In James's works neither option can categorically be denied a claim to legitimacy. In "Eugene Pickering" James raises, but does not resolve, a clash between modalities for appropriating life. Pickering chooses wrongly once in order that he may ultimately choose aright, gaining the experience of idealistic rapture in the process. The narrator remains a professional empathizer, unintrusive and chaste. But James has accorded the witness-narrator a full consciousness of the philosophy implicit in his natural posture as a narrator. "In retreat as it were, there must be the observer, the more compromised and less committed, the resister of extremity who from his middle existence can place extremity for us."[25] In this early Jamesian fable of initiation both the "plunger" and the "renouncer" have volitions and both experience an ever-expanding awareness. This, more than anything else, sets apart James's American variant from its Russian archetype.

More than James knew, his Pickering charts the same rite of passage, including even the same ambiguities, as does Turgenev's Sanin. One can imagine James proposing to himself the case of an *American* Sanin whose greatest temptation would not be sensual abandon, but the siren-song of Germanic transcendental ecstasy. But, as we have argued, the seduction plot in *Veshnie Vody* whirls around Gemma as well as around Polozova; the eruption of anarchic passion unshackles Sanin from the self-imposed confines of a spurious idyll. James, as we know, confused the image of Gemma with the more substantial, truly precious figures of Turgenev's virtuous heroines. As a result, James's American counterstatement to Turgenev's fable about a perfect provincial's ambivalent fall proves in the end to be a nearly parallel statement, an endorsement. The two fables of initiation, at the core of their ambiguous centers, are simultaneously profoundly antiromantic and deeply elegiac in lamenting the loss of an ennobling romantic exaltation of the human imagination. It is significant that the two stories locate the seat of illusion as well as the site of disenchantment in Europe or in images of it. In both, an ecstatic involvement with prefabricated cultural and artistic images is overcome, and "natural," "native" shapes of existence are embraced. If the tone of James's version of the situational predicament seems several shades lighter, it is not because the pathos of the initiation is any less intense. It is because we are not mired in the depression produced by the sorry spectacle of inert, articulate Russians. In James, the poignancy of lost illusions is as keen, but the innocent dupe at least marches on with the jaunty stride of American voluntarism. We retain the feeling that where there is at least a will, there is some cause for hope that there is a way out or a way back.

It can be argued that *Madame de Mauves* and "Eugene Pickering" are the first of James's many tales of American disenchantment with romantic mirages or "superstitious valuations" of Europe.[26] The archetypes for such fables of romantic "denitiation" are certainly available in Turgenev. But the extent to which Henry James perceived this particular dimension in Turgenev by 1873 is problematic. He tended to see in Turgenev's tales of experience a pessimistic dismissal of *all ideality*, showing it to be utterly cowed and brutalized by the dark empire of erotic force. Oddly, the Turgenev tales most upsetting to James in 1873 closely coincided in import with the countervailing American cases which James so deliberately conceived. Even the bleakest of Turgenev's songs of experience, that dismal tale of helpless self-victimization entitled "A Correspondence," does not portray a crushing victory of sensuality over ideality. If anything, it ironically bewails the disabling effects of an ineradicable sentimental streak in self-styled cosmopolitans. The philosophizing antihero, Alexei, is not brought low by raw, unidealized sexual appetites; he is seduced instead by the tinseled props of stagecraft in which an otherwise not very alluring ballerina seems a fatal Neapolitan beauty. Alexei's fall does not illustrate man's sure victimization by primitive eroticism; it demonstrates the tragicomic, self-victimizing plight of what the Germans call *der Kunst-Barbar*, the cultural barbarian or "culture hound." James's first readings of Turgenev missed the Russian's ambivalent, ironic affirmation of the hold superstitious valuations still had on men's minds. Upon closer acquaintance, the American would come to appreciate Turgenev's ambiguous postromantic cast of mind. In time, James would prove capable of closely following Turgenev's self-exposing first-person narrators. To anticipate a bit in pursuit of this contention, let us leap to 1879 and consider the James who devised "The Diary of a Man of Fifty."

The "Diary" is, for James, an unusual narrative experiment within the severe restrictions of the fictive autobiography. But contrary to a recent claim, it does not represent a *rare* instance of exploiting a narrator as an ironic center of self-revelation.[27] Most of James's early narratives emit warning signals to the reader over the heads of some rather unreliable narrators. In this particular case, the irony of the self-betrayal is especially cruel. The "Diary" purports to reconstruct the lived text of a twenty-seven-year-old Florentine romance as it is rehearsed in the mind of a British career officer of fifty-two. Ironically, if the text could be fully restored and impressed on young minds (as it very nearly is), it would thwart, not promote, faith in amorous bliss. For our officer, in his very first diary entry, stands self-revealed (if not self-recognized) as a campaigner so cautious in charting an expeditious route through life that his greatest pleasures are disinterments of long-buried gambles. The narrator, as of 1874, has come through life with a tidy conscience and, in a keynote phrase not yet sufficiently parsed, with "happiness mitigated by impertinent conjectures." (390)[28] Almost exactly three years later the narrator will begin to comprehend that the conjectures spoiling his positive happiness were his dark, melodramatic suspicions of thirty years ago and not his constant, teasing imaginings of wedded bliss. James's narrative slowly, archly exposes the emotional wasteland left in the wake of the morally fastidious life led by a dirty-minded Anglo-Saxon. Here James records a life of renunciation that results in an impoverishment of life.

The nameless, otherwise unremarkable narrator into whose diary we are given a privileged glimpse does possess one striking mark of identification: he is a perfect distillation of the analogical imagination. His mind expands in denuded present moments, filling deserted scenes with the fixed shapes of prior experience. "My imagination makes a great circuit and comes back to the starting point." (390) It is the sort of mind that discovers a refined existence in dwelling upon exhumed presences from a dead past. That this power of nostalgia is something less than heroic is indicated by James's subversive challenges to the narrator's analogical tyranny. It surely bodes ill, for instance, that the resuscitated image of the narrator's youthful flame is first encountered beneath an "exuberant" statue of the goddess Pomona, a statue intact from the past except for the minor dismemberment of a tapering finger! This is the first foreshadowing of the comic position occupied by our narrator, whose analogous world never quite matches the given fictive reality. As Queenie Leavis has noted, the "Diary" observes one of James's favorite conventions, "the structure built on alternative selves," a device admirably suited "for conducting psychological exploration in dramatic form."[29] Whereas the narrator is willing to believe in the literary realities of true coincidences and true "doubles," the reader is educated to appreciate a typically Jamesian savoring of life's alternative instances. To illustrate this, we need brief recourse to the plot embedded in James's "Diary."

Initially, the narrator is tempted to foist his interpretation of his abortive romance with a widowed Italian countess upon a young, propertied compatriot, Stanmer, who is similarly involved with the widowed daughter of that very same countess. Circumstantial evidence has prodded the grizzled veteran to undertake what Stanmer charitably calls "an extraordinary responsibility in trying to put a man out of conceit of a woman who, as he believes, may make him very happy." (407) But at times the narrator is not so single-minded; part of him wishes to permit the younger generation to invent its own denouement. These moments of indecision reflect the soldier's unstated ambivalence over the appropriateness of his own action in discontinuing his Italian romance. Significantly, the more he perceives the resemblance between mother and daughter, the more he is enchanted by the daughter; and the more he admires her, the greater his efforts to persuade Stanmer to reproduce his own youthful solution to the problem. The self-serving protectiveness behind this campaign to create a "double" is variously signaled to the reader. James has built into his fictive situation some props that symbolically belie the narrator's perspective. In addition to the miniature allegory of the disfigured Pomona, there is the first probing interview with Stanmer that takes place beneath a "solemn blank-eyed Hermes, with wrinkles accentuated by the dust of ages." (397) Perhaps the most blatant warning signal to the reader is the pointed reference to the fact that both generations of morally-impugned countesses are named "Bianca." These "talking props" are seconded by some conversations that are interpolated in the diary. In her first reported encounter with the diarist, the young countess is busy refuting his evil-minded presuppositions. "She was not like that" is her intense reprimand to his assumption that the mother easily forgot the old romance. In addition to the daughter's corrected version of the old soldier's stories, the reader is also given increasingly frequent glimpses of a Stanmer who is being ironical at his mentor's expense. In fact,

55

when the narrator finally recounts his long-withheld worst suspicions of the mother and thanks his instinct for rescuing his honor, Stanmer reacts by agreeing that "instinct's everything," ironically quoting England's most notorious coward and sensualist, Falstaff. (419) The narrator could hardly have been more effectively discredited.

What gradually emerges from James's "Diary" is that same sad old story about how cultural stereotypes can impoverish life's rarely proffered opportunities. A militant Anglo-Saxon is repelled instinctively by the "ethic" of Italian widowhood, an ethic which encourages a frank hospitality toward the ongoing pulses of the life-force. The narrator is predisposed to find Italian females rather lax in decorum and moral sense. These presumptions surface in the diary notes which relate the narrator's first encounter with the young countess, "full of frankness and freedom, of that inimitable *disinvoltura* which in an Englishwoman would be vulgar, and which in her is simply the perfection of apparent spontaneity. But for all her spontaneity she's . . . a consummate coquette." (405) These tactfully expressed comments cloak a mistrust and even a fear of what passes for spontaneity in human conduct. The English soldiers's ingrained circumspection, his immediate distrust of any behavior that is ornamental and not plain, leads him to ascribe uncharitable motives ("she wanted—a rich, susceptible, credulous, convenient young Englishman established near her *en permanence*"), which in turn led him to a retrenchment from active engagements. (417) James's general, by virtue of his dedication to a narrow, suspicious decorum, stands self-revealed in his mid-fifties as a craven fool on life's field of opportunity. Even for Anglo-Saxons, however, there can be an alternative solution; but it requires a risk of faith. Stanmer voices this alternate, uncircumspect strategy in his brash concluding postscript. "A fig for all analogies unless you can find an analogy for my happiness"! (423) What still remains in doubt, though, is whether Stanmer's fortunate alternative conduct can safely be applied as a general rule for negotiating one's way through life happily. For if all analogies leak and cannot contain life, then no case is strictly comparable.

It just so happens that one of the two "superb things" of Turgenev's that James praised to Henley in the summer of 1878 was the French version of *The Diary of a Superfluous Man*.[30] Even if we keep in mind that James's personal copy was back in America, Turgenev's work can still be seen as the prototype and prod behind the production of James's 1879 "Diary." The situational parallels are too equivalent to be discounted. We have the same gradually unfolding self-exposure of an unreliable autobiographer who is recalling the lone abortive romance of his life. More strikingly, we have the rival presence of an alternative self—a successful suitor roughly analogous to, but crucially different from, the emotionally atrophied narrator. Finally, and most subtly, the defaults and waste that mar the narrator's career can be attributed to a stereotypical cast of mind coupled with an extreme self-protecting prudence in conduct.

Turgenev's superfluous man, Chulkaturin, has been elevated onto a shaky pedestal as the monumental archetype for all the deracinated intellectuals in modern Russian literature. More modestly he may be seen as Turgenev most likely saw him—as symptomatic of the ineffectual postidealist, preempiricist Russian intelligentsia of the 1840s. But how much of all this could James have seen in the rough outlines of translation? What could James have seen in Chulkaturin? In the reconstructed youth of Chulkaturin one sees a twenty-two-year-old "under internal lock and key," *vermeille à l'intérieur.* (227) Intimidated by the burdensome proprieties of a masochistically virtuous mother, secretly infatuated with the genial liberties taken by a weak father, the high-strung youth we confront is already a confirmed over-reactor who leads a heady vicarious life. Placed in proximity to a high official's pubescent daughter, he interprets every awkward flush as the roseate dawn of passion. Exposed to the unwelcome intrusion of a Petersburg prince, he imagines the worst has occurred and he vacillates between the equally unsociable extremes of a surly silence and surly sarcasms. His absurd jealousy finally culminates in a highly literary, highly farcical duel. Once the illustrious rival's threat has passed and the "first infatuation" is over, Chulkaturin awaits the melodramatic bliss of forgiving the shamed, penitent woman. But in the end the romantic heroine comes to accept the hand of an unprepossessing, self-obliterating devotee, a creature whose very cognomen, Bizmyonkov, etymologically announces his "nameless" anonymity *(bez imyon).* Ironically, Chulkaturin's true, unflattering "double," servile and unpretentious as he is, claims the prize. Superimposed on this tale of an abortive young romance is the personality of the fatally ill, older Chulkaturin, a personality marred by an excruciating split between a sentimental nostalgia and a callous cynicism. It is here in the highly characterized rendering of the narrative incidents that this tale's well-deserved reputation lies.

The mastery in Turgenev's *Dnevnik* is most evident in the linguistic and situational patterning that emphasizes the narrator's existential trap.[31] The dominant structure encasing the autobiography is an endless vacillation between mutually exclusive polarities. This structure is enacted meteorologically in the erratic shifts between March thaws and freezes which accompany the expansive and contractive attitudes toward life that alternate in the meditations of the terminally ill narrator. This same patterned vacillation is enacted by the very medium of expression: grammatically, lexically, rhetorically, Chulkaturin's style is the man himself. Any given diary entry fluctuates between effusion and disillusion (or vice-versa) and back again. The syntax is a garble of clumsy modulations, an anthology of disjunctive connectives like "that's beside the point" *(delo ne v tom)*, "better yet" *(luchshe)*, "to resume" *(vozvratimsya)*, and "be that as it may" *(kak by to ne bylo)*. Lexically, Chulkaturin's speech ranges from provincial elocutions and vulgarisms to poetic tropes; rhetorically, it spans the gamut from purple patches of declamation to crude epithets and "downward comparisons."[32] 'In short, the diary presents an unrefereed clash of two styles of excessive response—sentimentalism and cynicism. One can find exclamatory personifications of Nature which are rudely interrupted by self-conscious aphoristic sneers. "Sentimental effusions are just like licorice: at first you suck and it doesn't seem bad at all, but after a while your mouth gets awfully foul-tasting." (143) Just before his "exit" on April 1, the narrator has penned a valedictory outpouring of farewells, but these get checked by a sudden awareness of bookishness. "I seem to be composing a sentimental tale or finishing off a 'desperate' letter." (178) What is important here is not the self-judgment, but the interruption. What most typifies Chulkaturin is his inability to make a complete emotional contact; one part of him is forever disavowing the sentiments and speculations the other part heedlessly indulges.

What we can extract from the self-revealing stylistics of Turgenev's diarist is the precise configuration of a predicament. The older Chulkaturin, reflecting on the moment when the younger self first realized that "his" Liza was oblivious of him, comes up with a telltale inversion of a conventional metaphor. "My last hopes collapsed with a crack, just as a block of ice, pierced by the spring sun, suddenly splits into small splinters." (158) Notice that hopes are here associated with winter's frozen lifeless forms. This is appropriate, given the fact that Chulkaturin's aspirations are shaped so slavishly in the fixed images of literary convention. We are clearly intended to perceive the narrator's literary conditioning, if not from the fact that his diary so often invokes the "as they say" (*kak govoryat*) formula, then from his duel-second's curious remark about having had enough of "authors."[33] (168) Given Chulkaturin's life-denying literariness, one might expect the demolition of such hopes to signal a welcome release. But, in fact, the crushed illusions produce instead a phlegmatic, life-inhibiting cynicism. It is only in his last rally of consciousness that Chulkaturin can affirm, "Live, you who are alive!" In the case of Turgenev's diarist, the cost of illusion and the cost of disillusion add up to the same sum—a paralyzing reflexivity. Although Bizmyonkov is the narrator's "double," he does not represent an alternative self in the same way Stanmer does for James's diarist. In Turgenev, "superfluousness" is experienced as a fatality. There are alternative modes of behavior in the same situation, but none are live options for the experiencing subject. Henry James had imagined a similar case, but the vacillating central consciousness clearly holds itself accountable for its mistaken choices. Once again, the difference between the Russian and the American rendition of a parallel situation is James's affirmation of the voluntaristic principle.

Allowing for the American accent on private initiative, it is important to perceive the general congruence of vision developing between the young American and the old Russian master. Two characteristic features may be said to link together the Turgenevan and the Jamesian tale of initiation. First, the dramatic tension in the tales centers not on the "fall" itself (there is never much suspense about that for a careful reader), but on the interpreting consciousness. The reader gets involved by wondering how one ought to take the "denitiation" from romance into experience; the central problem is how to reckon the value of the achieved clarification of life. Second, this general predicament tends, with both authors, to be imagined concretely within the confines of a specific fable—the "international theme." Again and again, Europe, either as a mental construct or as a geographical setting, represents an alluring complex of aesthetic and subconscious yearnings normally repressed by the provincial consciousness. Europe bursts upon the ingenuous awareness like a Poundian image: "It is the presentation of such a 'complex' instantaneously which gives that sense of sudden liberation; that sense of freedom from time limits and space limits; that sense of sudden growth, which we experience in the presence of the greatest works of art."[34] In both the American and the Russian tales of experience, Europe is first perceived as a romantic image before it is finally apprehended as an avatar of experience itself. Europe, because of the inflated romantic currency it circulated at home, could serve Turgenev and James as the perfect backdrop to illuminate the tragicomic trauma of provincial self-bedazzlement. It is precisely this shared hinterland apprehension of Europe that justifies our convoking Turgenev's "Three Meetings" (1852) with James's "Four Meetings" (1877).[35]

Turgenev's *Tri Vstrechi* is, technically speaking, far more sophisticated than James's slim tale. As is appropriate to a reminiscence of incidental encounters, the reader is given only an elaborately casual, highly impressionistic account of what really transpires in the central anecdote. As in life, we intersect the paths of other fates *in medias res*; we are acutely conscious of not sounding all the depths of others' motivations; we lose touch without arriving at any conclusive knowledge of the consequences faced by others. To add further lifelike complications, Turgenev's narrator is marvelously contrived as an unreliable teller. Ostensibly narrating the tale of a fellow countrywoman deluded in romance, the narrator, as he pieces things together, reveals his own romantic delusions. The tale is, in short, an extended bit of gossip about a dupe told by a dupe whose foolishness is betrayed by the poses and mannerisms Turgenev incorporates into the teller's diction. The text of Turgenev's story is deliberately studded with literary allusions and with rhapsodic "pathetic fallacies" which hopelessly obscure an empirical sight of the mundane affairs under way.[36]

The leitmotif of *Tri Vstrechi* is the hunt, which begins as a perfectly ordinary pursuit of wildfowl in the environs of the backwater settlement of Glinnoe (*glina* in Russian is "clay") and ends up a quixotic quest for an ineffable image of happiness. By a strange quirk of fate, the narrator, a provincial man of leisure with some minor experience and some major affectations of European culture, has been the involuntary witness of several balcony scenes from an abortive grand opera romance conceived in the head of one of his fair compatriots. Having wandered far afield in his customary hunt and standing immobile one motionless, moon-bedazzled night in the garden of an abandoned hill-top estate, the narrator, already in a state of quivering anticipation, suddenly hears a chord struck on the manse piano followed by the strains of a feminine aria, *"Vieni, pensando a me segretamente."* Such is the prelude to the narrator's second meeting with an unknown Sorrento belle whose lyrics he had first heard one luxuriant Italian night when "the golden globes of heavy oranges, hidden amidst the interlacing leaves, now barely visible, now glistening brightly, ostentatiously displayed themselves in the moonlight." (182) On both occasions, the narrator stands impotently aside while a man of his general stature (but with an aquiline nose and magnificent mustaches) enters the private chambers of this "Psyche," this "Galatea." Frustrated in his attempts to deduce the identity of the songstress, the huntsman tries first to cajole, then to bribe the impassive old custodian of the estate, but he refuses to believe what he is told—that only two rather elderly ladies have returned to the manse. Ridden by a romantic quest, Turgenev's normally befuddled narrator dreams a revelatory dream. First he sees his love take flight from a desert waste singing "Addio . . . why hast thou not wings?" Transformed next into a cloud, she is enmeshed in the threads of a lascivious sun. Outraged, the dream-narrator shouts, "That is not the sun, that is not the sun; it is an Italian spider. Who gave it a passport to Russia? I'll show him up for what he is: I saw him stealing oranges from other people's gardens." (186) In the final dream sequence, faced by a perpendicular cliff and taunted by his beloved's aria, *"Passa quei colli,"* the narrator's knightly charge gets thwarted by the old serf-custodian, who now appears as a jealous Don Quixote who will not bear anyone's attaining *his* Dulcinea. In the nightmare's finale, the narrator's heart is fatally pierced, significantly enough, *by Don Quixote's lance.* After this masterfully executed dream, Turgenev could rest assured that the reliability of his waking narrator had been permanently discredited. To emphasize the point, he has his narrator admit that he often misses quail because he cannot whistle "objectively" enough. (191)

The single most reliable indicator of the depths behind the tale's anecdote is provided by Turgenev's skillfully deployed language. The speaker compulsively reiterates the adverb "motionlessly" *(nepodvizhno)*, yet his natural vocabulary is that of the hunt. The Russian *okhota* (hunt) and its companion term *okhotnik* (hunter) have a double meaning which is fully exploited in Turgenev's text; the former can also mean "impulse" or "urge" and the latter either "lover" or "zealot." Thus, the linguistic pattern of the narrative is such that it constantly suggests to the reader the paradoxical notion of a motionless hunt, of a quest immobilized—and this, of course, is the inner plot behind the sporadic action of the anecdote. One of the few occasions on which the narrator takes some initiative elicits a pregnant comment from the most important commentator within the story. The narrator prevails upon the stern old custodian to show him through the abandoned manse; when he finally invades the old man's special preserve, the storeroom with its gallery of gloomy ancestral portraits, the custodian plaintively grumbles: "Da, chto vam za *okhota*"—"Do you really want to bother?" (194) Later this same storeroom becomes the scene of the old man's apparently unmotivated suicide; actually, his self-destruction functions as a symbolic act of protest against the violation of old world values and decorum. And in the final bitterly ironic encounter, Turgenev's persistent pun on the hunt motif surfaces again. The narrator overtakes his "Galatea" at a masquerade ball soon after she has been jilted by her European partner who, presumably, has finally wearied of operatic scenes. But now that his Dulcinea figure is so accessible, the narrator's inner check comes to the fore. Faced with the remnants of a mundane affair, the quest ends and the romance dissipates. It is now that the narrator weakly confesses, "Ya ne *okhotnik* predavat'sia bezumnym nadezhdam"—"I am not fond of pursuing senseless hopes." (201) At the end, the European male, "a rather enigmatic individual," slips away with an insolent smirk on his lips. *Tri Vstrechi* is a very polished rendition of one more episode in what the reader must assume is the on-going victimization of provincials by their own all-too-literary image of European experience.

Henry James's "Four Meetings," being more widely known to American readers, will require no such detailed treatment. What should be obvious is that this pathetic story of the culturally deprived schoolmistress, Miss Caroline Spencer, and her arty cousin is also an ironic depiction of imperceptive provincial ingénues. Compared to Turgenev's treatment of a similar theme, this early James story is more patently ironic; it is much more a single lucid anecdote and much less sophisticated in its exploration of the dramatic method. The narrator is obviously and annoyingly the master of the situation to which he is witness. He is unlikeably smug and fastidious, what with his savoring the role of titillating New England damsels with photographs of Europe and his readiness to beat a retreat in good order when any enthusiasms get out of control. In short, this narrator's objectivity is purchased by forfeiting his involvement in the anecdote. James's narrator is not the dupe that Turgenev's is, yet his aloofness and neutrality, his reluctance to interfere, make him an unaware victimizer of the tragicomic heroine.

James more closely approximates Turgenev in emulating the theme of the involuntary quester who stubbornly recoils from any witting contact with the mundane. As in Turgenev, the dupe's malfunctioning vision can be attributed to a whole culture's astigmatism. Miss Spencer is fondly accused of bearing "the native American passion—the passion for the picturesque" which is "primordial—antecedent to experience. Experience comes and only shows us something we have dreamt of." (92) Also as in Turgenev, the provincial's stereotype of European romance is exploited by worldly Continentals to the ultimate victimization of any hinterlander whose imagination is starved and bookish. In this regard it is only fair to note that Miss Spencer's sombrero-flourishing cousin is no less duped than the naïve maiden relative he literally cheats of the means to see all Europe. He is made to pay a price for dreaming the Bohemian dream; as villain and as visionary, he is pathetically banal.

Grimwater, U.S.A., like Glinnoe in Russia, proves that wherever the native soil is most culturally depleted and most hostile to the imagination, there it is that the strangest shoots of fancy thrive. The subtlest touches in James's story act to heighten our awareness of the parasitic relationship between Miss Spencer's incurable romanticism and Grimwinter's parsimonious Protestant ethic. Deeply ingrained in Caroline Spencer is an inner censor which regards active leisure or realized indulgences as "impure satisfactions," but which, by fostering acts of renunciation, can lend a good conscience to the most foolish of vicarious fancies. Thus it is that a New England Puritan can conscientiously subsidize what she deems "a wonderful old world romance" so long as she herself is willing to scrimp and deny in paying for the upkeep of cherished delusions. As in Turgenev, a faultily romanticized Europe is the perfect vehicle for bringing home to the reader the message of life's quotidian reality. But, pathetically, there will always be those like Miss Spencer who refuse to be initiated, who refuse to let their refined senses touch the stuff of life. The deluded schoolmistress has given house room to a vulgar and cheap imitation of *haute couture* and high culture; she can no longer afford to meet the real thing.[37]

"When are you going to Europe again?"
This question seemed brutal; but there was something that irritated me in the softness of her resignation, and I wished to extort from her some expression of impatience.
She fixed her eyes for a moment upon a small sun-spot on the carpet; then she got up and lowered the window-blind a little, to obliterate it. Presently, in the same mild voice, answering my question, she said—"Never!" (110)

In sum, the two tales of intercontinental meetings both unfold the tragicomic spectacle of provincial self-victimization before romantic images of Europe. In both, experience and life are impoverished by willingly imperceptive viewers of the scene. But other outcomes resulting from intercultural transplantation are surely imaginable. The provincial need not necessarily be the dupe. A worldly individual might be too realistic, too skeptical about the possible varieties of human experience. In such cases an individual could cheat himself of a balanced diet of life by being too wary and too wise.

One such case is Winterbourne, whose thwarted heliotropic growth toward light and innocence is the central drama in Henry James's single most famous story, "Daisy Miller" (1878).[38] A suggestively similar case, as yet unnoticed, is the wistful bachelor who collects reminiscences and dried geraniums and narrates Turgenev's *Asya* (1858). The juxtaposition of these two tales takes on greater plausibility when one reflects that both are "international" fables in which a pure native maiden is grossly misconstrued by a Europeanized compatriot. There is a common *donnée*: to situate two manifestations of provincialism (nativist ignorance and cosmopolitan snobbery) next to one another in the heart of an inoffensive, unoffending Europe. Such structural and situational parallels can be reinforced by circumstantial evidence mustered from literary history. Turgenev's tale appeared in an American translation as "Assja" in 1877. Moreover, this was published in *Galaxy*, to which Henry James frequently contributed articles. Thus in 1877, James might well have been reminded of the French translation he first read in the Hetzel volume of 1869, *Nouvelles Moscovites*. In that edition, Turgenev's title heroine was rechristened "Annouchka" (little Anna). Informed by this context, it is an intriguing detail James gives us when he drops reference to the fact that Daisy's real name is Annie P. Miller. This is the sort of literary detail that prods a further investigation. What, besides a shared name, do the two heroines have in common?

The entrance of a young woman in a Turgenevan tale marks a pivotal moment in the dramatic structure of the fiction. Specifically, it represents the incursion of a romantic, extrinsic force which is capable of violating the environmental norms, but which is generally contained at last by the mundane setting.[39] Surely the pathos of such a bittersweet fate applies equally well to Daisy Miller as to Asya. To cite another parallel, the unconventionality of each heroine is finally stifled by sympathizing male protagonists who nonetheless embody the momentum of societal inertia. The opening, self-characterizing lines of

Tales of Initiation (1874-79)

Turgenev's anonymous narrator evoke a presence remarkably similar to that of Winterbourne. We meet a foot-loose but singularly unfanciful traveler in his mid-twenties, someone economically well-fixed and physically well-favored. This bachelor is profoundly unattached; respectably aimless, he wanders abroad in pursuit of neither learning nor love, but simply because he "felt like looking over God's world." (164)[40] Despite his occasional familiarity with "studies" and with older foreign ladies, he is instinctively a paragon of level-headed prudence. Turgenev's narrator is, in brief, a virtually exact precursor of James's Geneva watch in the guise of an American male. Our Russian bachelor's tastes are carefully, calculatingly delineated in Turgenev's text, for they are psychically revealing. We are given a young man who is constitutionally averse to sublime prospects. Although sensitive to nature, he cannot tolerate an obtrusive landscape filled with "so-called beauty spots: unusual heights, cliffs and waterfalls." (164) In literature as in landscape, he prefers an unruffled bucolic atmosphere; he reads aloud the idyllic Goethe of *Hermann und Dorothea* and gratefully apostrophizes: "Hail modest nook of German land with your unsophisticated content, your omnipresent traces of diligent hands and patient, unhurried toil!" (178) We are dealing with a personality that permits itself enthusiasms, provided they are expressed in "tears of abstract ecstasy." (186) This is the sort of sentimental psyche that fears the concentrated force of the directed libido, the sort that finds a protective nook in the proprieties. Under threat, such timid "decent" folk have been known to hallucinate some darkly picturesque scenes. In any case, Turgenev's socially correct antihero, exactly like Winterbourne, maintains his fastidious limitations on actual experience by indulging in vicarious and dark imagination. Hardheaded realism is here a ruse for keeping life at an unhealthy remove. Basically the creature in question is meek. But a sentimental psyche, once cornered and on the defensive, can be cruel and savage.[41] Not surprisingly, Winterbourne and his Russian counterpart, who share similar cowardices, recoil from feminized embodiments of life that strongly resemble one another.

Addicted to observing and analyzing the varieties of feminine beauty from a properly appreciative distance, Winterbourne is lured into a risky intimacy with Daisy by the "the mystery of the young girl's sudden familiarities and caprices." (167) Turgenev's insatiably curious but usually stolid people-watcher is similarly allured by Asya's sprite-like physical and psychic agility. "I had never seen a more mobile being." (168) Both maidens charmingly embody the principle of improvisation amidst a setting firmly regulated by the tyranny of custom. Asya, who has voluntarily perched herself on the sublime heights of a mountain eyrie, is quite literally represented as a daring bounder on ancient ledges, an act which is but the physical analogue to her penchant for overleaping traditional social circles. In all this, she is a forecast of the impudently innocent Daisy who walks the hoary streets of Italy in questionable company. Our two improvisatrices are also closely related in the motive force that drives their kaleidoscopic display of effects. Both wish to provoke or cajole an uncustomary response, a token gesture of inner agitation, from the walking monuments of civility it is their misfortune to admire. In both instances the amorous intrigue symbolically evokes the larger drama of civilization cruelly banishing its malcontents. Beyond even this, one can cite a stronger confirmation that Asya and Daisy are legitimately related literary kinfolk.

The uninhibited naturalness that both girls exemplify is deliberately presented as the quintessential poetry of each girl's homeland. Asya is as purely and fetchingly "Russian" as Daisy is, in her little brother's appropriate introduction, "an American girl." In both cases the girl's typical national spirit is the *author's* pure poetry and is not necessarily shared by the narrator or by contemporary readers.[42]   Turgenev's bachelor considers Asya most Russian when she takes on the aspect of the Old Russian maiden—meek, self-effacing, virtually serflike. (174-75) In fact, though, it is the mercurial, lofty-living Asya who represents Turgenev's pure poetry of an integral Russianness. The evidence for this is unmistakable. Asya voices her wish to be identified with Tatyana, Pushkin's ideal model of spontaneous, virtuous Russian womanhood. (185) And in her own right Asya is the "natural" daughter of an aristocratic widower and a sternly Orthodox servant maid. In short, Asya is the imagined composite of a divided culture, a poetic forecast of a unified Russian spirit. The very torment of divided loyalties that she undergoes as a result of her "false position" also spurs her imagination to encompass bold visions "to go somewhere far, as in a procession, to accomplish a difficult, wondrous feat." (184) But instead of a crusader or a saint (the kind of companion her metaphors envisage), it is Turgenev's narrator who crosses her path. It is after their initial meeting that Asya, with an unwitting prescience, observes, "You crossed into the column of moonlight; you've shattered it." (169) Daisy Miller as she is being escorted from the moonlit Coliseum in the company of Winterbourne's black thoughts might well have said the same!

Who, then, is to blame in these tragicomedies in which the knock of opportunity at the door goes unheard? The authors imply answers in the narrative refraction of each situation. The strategy of tale-telling is the same. The reader is allowed to overhear a voice of experience as it recites its first encounter with a true song of innocence. But it is only when the score is finished that we understand the "conductor" was incapable of recognizing the authentic notes of innocence when he heard them. We are made witnesses to a stupid fatality. We become frustrated bystanders as the forces of conditioning score a dumb victory over the ingenuous and ingenious human imagination. The two victimized parties suffer from a fatal and a fated unawareness. Daisy is fatally insouciant. Her midnight rendezvous in the Coliseum was sure fodder for the mangling mills of social gossip; besides, it was medically unhealthy. So, too, Asya's bold initiative in arranging a tryst was bound to terrify even those who were normally relaxed about the proprieties, let alone a male so conventional as to be sensitive about the "irregularity" of her handwriting. (189) The two stories are deeply congruent in the wistful, complexly ironic awareness the presiding imaginations have to offer us. Both tales imply a restrained refusal to endorse either internalized or externalized criteria for social conduct. Both authors record a fatal collision between nativist and cosmopolitan behavioral standards without venturing to predict the probability of a dialectical synthesis.[43] The basic structure makes a basic cautionary point. Having witnessed the pathetic stalemate that results when the realistic and the romantic imaginations foreclose on one another's intuitions about life, might not the reader be apt to expand the normal hospitality of his own imagination? The same design lurks behind the spectacle of wasted affections in *Asya* and in "Daisy Miller." Two mutually exclusive life-styles have been given similar fictional embodiments in the histories of *Asya* and the bachelor, of Daisy Miller and Winterbourne. And the completed anecdote in each testifies to the sacrifice of life that is the cost of foreclosing one's imagination to experiential possibilities.

It would contradict the spirit as well as the intent of this study to claim exclusive rights for Turgenev as James's sovereign inspiration in "Daisy Miller" or, for that matter, in articulating the "international theme." The young James was a voracious reader and an incorrigible traveler; he had assimilated many sophisticated devices into his well-stockpiled literary imagination. From internal evidence as well as assiduous scholarship, it has become evident that "Daisy Miller" derives, in the particulars of its setting, from Cherbuliez's *Paule Méré*, which first located Geneva as the spiritual center for conventions constricting enough to stifle an innocently frank and fresh young lady.[44] Likewise, the growing body of criticism on the "international theme" is progressively complicating the likely sources (as well as any plausible definition) of that specific fable.[45] But what matters most for our purpose is the congruence of root implications that can be extracted from any given fable shared by Turgenev and James. In any final analysis the "international theme," however defined, must be seen as a structural variation on the "transplantation" or "intrusion" plots common to traditional comedy and satire.[46] Moreover, the genealogy of the international fable is only of skin-deep concern compared with the temperamental and visionary affinities that constitute the sort of influence I would prefer to chart. At most, the international fable is but a means for graphically locating and localizing a conflict that is, in the Turgenevan and Jamesian tales of initiation, a placeless, timeless predicament.

Underneath the topicality and the typicality of these narratives about provincial culture-seekers, Turgenev and James are engaging the selfsame paradigm of experience. Both authors manipulate situationally similar "intrusion" plots toward tragicomic, rather than purely comic, conclusions. With elaborate virtuosity these kindred imaginations envisage in fictions over and over again the lost adventures in life. There is a marked concern for all the missed excursions that have departed forever as a sad natural consequence of the fact that man habitually permits prior conceptualizations to anticipate experience. Both imaginations also envisage a world in which pain accompanies an expansion in consciousness as naturally as it does an expansion in physique. Some of these tales of maturation are primarily narratives of initiation in which the cost of dullness and imperceptiveness is reckoned. Others are more properly called narratives of denitiation in which the price of a prolonged adolescence figures large. Still others, perhaps the best, combine the two themes in counterpoint, presenting the painful paradoxical irony that the "tough-minded" and the "tender-minded" alike pay a human sacrifice to maintain their conceptualizations of experience.

Tales of Initiation (1874-79)

In the young James, at least initially, there was a hesitation to ascribe a bleak fatality to a character's becoming ensnared in culturally conditioned responses. Slowly, though, the role of ineluctable contingency, even in the most brilliant of careers, was recognized. The Henry James who wrote the first short masterpieces already shared with Turgenev a nontechnical intuition concerning the shape of provincial experience far more seminal in its influence than any situational or structural parallelisms that can be cited as the props of a literary influence.

Henry James gradually uncovered his deepest temperamental and "subtextual" affinities with Ivan Turgenev as he experimented with situational parallels in tales of initiation, especially those predicated on an "international" *donnée*. But as the James of the 1909 "Prefaces" reminds us, the major interest even in the early fables was not in fashioning literary daguerrotypes of cis-Atlantic travelers. However profitable a vein of literary ore it was, James's international theme was tapped more by default than by desire. "Given, after this fashion, my condition of knowledge, the most general appearance of the American [of those days] in Europe, that of being almost incredibly *unaware of life*—as the European order expressed life—had to represent for me the *whole* exhibitional range."[47] In short, the international tale provides a good beginning, an initial mode of expression; it was an illustrative convenience meant to imply a much vaster paradigm of "innocent" encounters with experience. For a glimpse of that wider exhibitional range and an estimate of Turgenev's impact on it, we must turn next to the larger canvases of James's first apprenticeship novels.

CHAPTER FIVE

Turgenev's Art of The Novel

Ivan Turgenev has become the oldest of the Russian Old Masters, a delicate and rather dusty literary curio brought out on brief exhibit in courses and tables of contents.[1] Yet in the America of Howells and James, the Ireland of George Moore, the Italy of Giovanni Verga, the name of Ivan Turgenev figured prominently in excited accounts of recent innovations in the craft of fiction. Significantly, Turgenev's most responsive readers and critics were themselves realists and provincials who were struggling to express the sensibility and experience of Europe's peripheral cultures. In this brief chapter, I want to suggest that the current insensitivity to the unique structural properties of Turgenev's novels may stem from our having outgrown an appreciation for the complex implications of a perspective on human experience that is both refined and alertly provincial. The novels of Ivan Turgenev once exported internationally, and most especially to America, the encouraging notion that a heightened provincial consciousness could be a distinguished possession as well as a sad token of impoverishment.

Before Turgenev the novelist had come into being, Turgenev the literary and cultural commentator was posing some very American questions about the future of the novel in a socially underdeveloped culture. Anyone remotely acquainted with Henry James's famous catalogue of America's cultural disadvantages in his *Hawthorne* volume of 1879 will recognize a familiar condition being aired in Turgenev's 1852 review of a Russian literary monstrosity now mercifully forgotten. "What can one fill four volumes with? . . . it is pertinent to ask now whether the basic elements of our social life have articulated themselves sufficiently to provide the material for a quadripartite novel."[2] Neither Turgenev nor James embarked on a career as novelist without first recognizing that the "life" they specifically knew could not compete in density or volume of experience with the available narrative models in European social fiction. Neither writer seriously hoped to emulate the giant and intertwined canvases of a Balzac or a Dickens. To be "realistic" about the way provincial nationalities might experience and articulate their felt identities, that was the immediate narrative challenge. It posed a problem which would clearly require some meddling with the size and structure of what passed for "the novel" in Europe.

Turgenev was himself hesitant to categorize his six most ambitious prose works as novels. When originally published, only his last and lengthiest narrative, *Virgin Soil*, was explicitly labeled a novel *(roman)*; the author identified all the others as extended tales *(bol'shie povesti).*[3] Beneath this seeming inconsistency on Turgenev's part lay some interesting and cogent considerations. Perhaps by juxtaposing Turgenev's two most programmatic formulations of his kind of novel we can bring into focus the issues of substance that lay behind the terminological vacillation.

First, consider Turgenev's well-known defensive response to his rival in Russian social fiction, that specialist in grand prose panels, Ivan Goncharov. "Whoever is in need of a novel in the epic sense, that person will not need me: I would as soon think of creating a novel as of walking on my head: no matter what I write, my work will always take the form of a series of sketches."[4] But compare that with the following *profession de foi* from Turgenev's foreword to the 1880 edition of his collected *novels (romany):*[5]

> In the course of all this time I have been aiming, insofar as my strength and intelligence have sufficed, conscientiously and impartially to depict and embody in suitable types what Shakespeare calls "the body and pressure of time" and the quickly changing physiognomy of Russians of the cultured stratum, which has served preeminently as the object of my observations.

An immediate tension is established when the two statements of summation confront one another. To invoke comparison with the gallery of types from Shakespeare's history plays is to betray an imagination with epic ambitions, just the sort of imagination seemingly discountenanced by Turgenev in mid-career. But surely it is unnecessary to deny the epic scope of Turgenev's imagination simply because he so consistently refused to compose narratives of epic proportions. What is necessary is to imagine the Turgenevan novel as fundamentally "a series of sketches" which yet manages to be somehow epic in scope. As Richard Freeborn has suggested, "his novels infer [sic] epic issues despite their structural resemblance to short stories."[6]

Still, by what structural legerdemain can a Turgenev "chamber novel" imply an epic dimension of reference? Some assistance, I think, can be garnered from Marvin Mudrick's observation that narratives of novella length "are likely to approach the conditions of poetry . . . The shorter the work of fiction, the more likely are its characters to be simply functions and typical manifestations of a precise and inevitable sequence of events."[7] Turgenev's characters are, of course, larger and richer than mere symbolic functions, but it is true that they take on individuality and suprapersonal significance within a narrative form that is concise enough to sketch a chamber drama, a domestic intrigue. The curious intermediate length of the Turgenevan novellalike novel is itself suggestive of a process of poetic condensation. The peculiar confines of this novelistic form permit Turgenev to execute characterizations which are intermediate between "types" ensnared in paradigmatic actions and "personalities" embroiled in idiosyncratic careers. Turgenev was himself quite aware of a subtle balance to be striven for in the creation of striking and significant characters. In 1874, to the delight of Howells and James, Turgenev confided to an enterprising Cornell professor of literature the secrets of his technique of characterization. After describing his famous system of compiling elaborate dossiers on "deployable" individuals, Turgenev went on to proclaim:[8]

> I seldom find it suitable to my purpose to copy directly a person of my own acquaintance, because it is but rarely that one finds a pure type. I then ask myself what nature intended with this or that person, what this or that trait of character would be if developed to its last pyschological consequences. . . . I endeavor not to give undue prominence to any one trait; even if ever so characteristic, I try to show my men and women *en face* as well as *en profile*.

Notice that Turgenev's imagination respects the expressive potential of a given concrete personality, but poetically expands upon those capacities to arrive at a symptomatic figure, yet one not wholly deprived of the original being's contrarieties. I would like to call this process "typification" to distinguish it from the notion of the literary "type" central to European Realism from Hippolyte Taine to Georg Lukacs.[9] The point is that Turgenev's characterological strategy was inductive; his imagination did *not* move in the direction of fleshing out, or concretizing, metahistorical concepts. Incidentally, the relevance of Turgenev's compositional procedure to the presentation of character in Henry James's early novels is striking. According to Richard Poirier's careful summation, the young James's self-conscious goal was "to avoid sacrificing the complexity or richness of character in the interest of moral edification or the representation of abstract qualities," but simultaneously "to avoid subverting the emblematic qualities of the characters by overly strenuous psychological definition of motive."[10] As in so much else, this particular American dilemma of characterization was helped toward artistic resolution by the persuasive example of Ivan Turgenev's "provincial" artistry.

Several large assertions have now been advanced. First, that Turgenev's manner of typifying his novelistic protagonists is unusual and that this process helps account for the peculiar narrative size of his *romany*. Second, the Turgenevan novel is said to display consistently a subtle genius for transforming a sketch of private relations, an intimate fictional *affaire*, into a public symbol of large cultural dynamics. We shall want to investigate how Turgenev's typifications operate to create an epic frame of reference. But at this juncture, it is my intent to reconnoiter some other important structural peculiarities of the novel as conceived by Ivan Turgenev.

There is a recurring formulaic structure within the basic fable that constitutes the central symbolic action in Turgenev's six novels. To be appreciated, this structural formula has to be set beside the core fable one encounters in the great European "novels of apprenticeship." Put simply, Turgenev tells a different story. Put more fashionably, Turgenev does not write a standard *Bildungsroman*. Since Lionel Trilling has gracefully avoided the technical term while lucidly explicating the essence of the matter, we can use him as our guide. The kind of novel the provincial realist, Turgenev, did not write, oddly enough, is the narrative of apprenticeship whose "defining hero may be known as the Young Man from the Provinces." Here, in capsule, is his story:[11]

He need not come from the provinces in literal fact, his social class may constitute his province ... Thus equipped with poverty, pride, and intelligence, the Young Man from the Provinces stands outside life and seeks to enter. ... It is the fate of the Young Man to move from an obscure position into one of considerable eminence in Paris or London or St. Petersburg, to touch the life of the rulers of the earth. ... That the Young Man be introduced into the great houses and involved with large affairs is essential to his story. ... Unlike the merely sensitive hero, he is concerned to know how the political and social world are run and enjoyed; he wants a share of power and pleasure and in consequence he takes real risks, often of his life.

Within this general schema of a realistic drama of initiation, numerous outcomes are readily imaginable, but reality itself is fairly strictly understood to require personal development and eventual maturation in the direction of *social* integration. "The *Bildungsroman* has tended to portray the education of a *would-be* artist, a young man who comes to his senses, ceases to dabble in areas in which he discovers he has no talent, and associates himself with some useful activity in the social community."[12] Even from such a brief excursion around the "great tradition" of the European novel of apprenticeship, we can carry back some far-ranging insights. Consider the formal implications of this core fable. Any novel predicated on these elements must be densely representational in setting, picaresque in plot, epic in scope. The Young Man from the Provinces is conceived of as an initial nonentity, a blank page, possessing no semblance of culture, no inherent status *as* a provincial. His ultimate fate, his completed identity takes shape only through the elaborate etching on his most impressionable skin by a complex social machinery. The career of such a protagonist cannot be other than the record of a protracted evolution, requiring many pages in the telling and much plotting in the process. It is obvious that Turgenev, who also wrote narratives about provincials learning about life, nevertheless told a different story. Why was that?

Two perceptive comments by V. S. Pritchett help to illuminate the unique shape of Turgenev's novels of apprenticeship. First, Pritchett has noted that Bazarov's whole problem in life is not so much the notorious generation gap of "fathers and children" as that Turgenev placed him in the country instead of in the city. Second, Pritchett generally remarks in Russian writers "a humility before the important fact of human inertia, the half-heartedness of its wish to move and grow, its habit of returning into itself."[13] These two revelations suggest, I think, a further revelation that is most important: the structural formula for

Turgenev's core novelistic fable is the exact obverse, the complete reversal, of the recurring fable in the European *Bildungsromanen*. Turgenev's imagination, informed by a sense of provincial realism, compulsively reenacts a basic scenario which calls for the injection, or more commonly the return, of an ex-provincial protagonist into the heartland of what Turgenev labels, in the last words of his last novel, *Bezymiannaia Rus'*, "Anonymous Russia." In *Rudin* (1856), the central action takes place in or near the Lasunskaya estate, "a huge brick structure erected in accordance with Rastrelli sketches in the taste of the last century ... at the foot of which flowed one of the chief rivers of Central Russia." (II) And in *Virgin Soil* (1876), the would-be revolutionaries actively shuttle between that dark and obscure "forest," the Russian folk, and the well-regulated suburban Sipyagin estate where the master, in between the imperious ringings of a Chinese dinner gong and the garrisonlike calls of night watchmen, ludicrously announces "the major motto of our house is freedom." Even the one glaring exception to the expected Turgenev setting is not quite so atypical. Although *Smoke* (1866) takes place largely in Baden-Baden, the hero's central involvement is a near-fatal amorous entanglement with a heroine whose very being springs from, and seductively embodies, the immemorial, instinctual "darkness" of Russia.[14] By one means or another, Turgenev always contrives to send his fictional "apprentices" into enigmatic and often primitive country to get schooled in life. And what happens next, happens with formulalike frequency in Turgenev's novels.

In one of the very few "Formalist" studies of the composition of Turgenev's novels, Vasili Gippius outlined the regular dynamic pattern which drove the central action forward. "The hero, appearing in what is for him a new milieu, struggles with it and, evincing a more or less noticeable influence on it, himself undergoes influences on its part."[15] More specifically, the hero's clash with the environment coincides with his meeting a heroine who emerges from that same milieu; that meeting is the catalyst for the central love intrigue, the unraveling of which usually finds the hero separated again, either restlessly wandering or dead. To this, Richard Freeborn would add one more specific. "In each case it is the ideas proferred by the hero that seem to have the major appeal to the heroine. For these ideas are the product of a different social experience, a different education, a different conditioning and the heroine is attracted to the newness of these ideas."[16] Boiling down the elements in the chemistry of a Turgenevan love intrigue we find that a relatively exotic "ideological" hero is brought into touch with an indigenous heroine who is an overreacher in her environment, an idealist or even a spiritualist like Liza in *A Nest of Gentryfolk*. In Marianna of *Virgin Soil* we glimpse the epitome of the Turgenev heroine. "Marianna belonged to a special order of unfortunate beings (in Russia one rather frequently encounters them nowadays) for whom justice is satisfying, but not elating, while injustice, to which they are terribly sensitive, jolts them in their innermost depths." (XIII) Typically, the Turgenevan scenario calls for the separation of the volatile, mutually-attracted elements; they usually prove to be totally incompatible once suspended in the resident culture surrounding them.

Our schematic model of the basic fable underlying *any* Turgenev novel closely corresponds to Oscar Cargill's generic definition of an "international novel"—"a character, usually guided in his actions by the mores of one environment, is set down in another, where his learned reflexes are of no use to him, where he must employ all his individual resources to meet successive situations, and where he must intelligently accommodate himself to the new mores, or in one way or another be destroyed."[17] For Cargill, the textbook illustration of this formula is James's *The American* (1877). Yet, except for the fact that the backdrop is not international, the same schema perfectly describes what happens to Bazarov in *Fathers and Sons*. Indeed, all of Turgenev's novels, regardless of setting, hinge dramatically upon what is essentially an international confrontation in Cargill's sense of that term—"a true clash of character based on mores."[18] The core fable in a Turgenev novel is a very particular subspecies of "intrusion plot."

Basically, a Turgenev novel tells the tragicomic tale of "an intruder in the dust"; it relates his dramatic reception and his equally dramatic rebuff by what is, metaphorically, the core of the earth, Mother Earth's heartland. The pun on Faulkner's title is deliberate; the imagination of the creator of works like *The Hamlet* was intimately attuned to the special world of Turgenev. To continue, though, an "intruder" in a Turgenev novel need not be a total stranger, a foreigner; more commonly, the intruding hero is a local who has gone astray—a voluntary absentee or an internal emigré. The "dust" which is intruded upon is a vast symbolic entity; it refers to all manifestations in Turgenev of what Pritchett calls the Russian humility before the "important fact of inertia" at the earth's core. When especially oppressive, it becomes that substance in which all aspirations, all exhortations get mired—mud. The great and central natural force to be conjured with by Turgenev's aspiring earth-shakers from the provinces is ever the same—the force of inertia.

At the opening of the second chapter of *Fathers and Sons*, the homecoming university graduate, Arkady, genially remarks, "Let me shake myself, papa, I am soiling you all over." Arkady means to be considerate. But if the gesture is a simple one, its verbal associations are not. There is a subtle undertone of generational aggression here. Arkady is politely warning his father, in ringing youthful accents *(zvonkim iunosheskim golosom)*, that he is unwittingly "soiling" his sire in his impetuous enthusiasm. The verb used, *zapachkat'*, also carries with it the associated idea of "staining" or "besmirching" reputations. So a vague, but operative, tension is present in this first light-hearted generational encounter. But in the total context of *Fathers and Sons* a cruel irony is perpetrated. It is Bazarov, the standard-bearer of the youthful contingent, who is soiled and finally buried; and Arkady's loftiest aspirations have to be, as it were, "grounded" in the earthy soil of Russian farm life. This "grounding" process is what invariably happens to all the Turgenevan enthusiasts and ideologues who intrude upon "the dust." Those who cannot accustom themselves to hard tillage and toil simply perish like Turgenev's first and last inspirational preachers, Rudin and Nezhdanov. And even those willing to labor the earth, like Lavretsky or Litvinov, never do make themselves at home on native soil. All the intruder protagonists end their careers as spiritual waifs and wanderers, as *stranniki* or *skitaltsy*.

Problems of transport, as in the last interview with Rudin before his exodus abroad, take on large symbolic implications. In Turgenev's Russia it is difficult to get anyplace. Even in *Smoke*'s rather optimistic conclusion, real progress is not spared a withering irony. "Fortunately, it turns out that among us in Russia one can travel quite nicely, even with a shattered wheel and especially, over the 'soft spots'—that's to say, through the muck." (XXVIII) It seems indisputable that the presiding spirit over Turgenev's Mother Russia is Uncle Uvar Ivanych, that enigmatic, hulking, and virtually immobilized giant who looms large enough to becloud the concluding promise of *On The Eve*. Not by chance is Uncle Uvar Turgenev's single most allegorized figure. The novel's resident artist, the perceptive sculptor, Shubin, strives to convince us that this human mound really *is* "the force of the black earth—the cornerstone of the social structure" in the flesh. (VIII) Turgenev elevates this seriocomic figure to the status of a virtual earth-deity or folk oracle. Always cryptic and practically inarticulate, great Uvar's answer to the urgent question, "When will *real* people exist?" is a wriggling of his fingers and an "It shall be." In other words, "in God's own good time." Such is the actual time schedule for true accomplishment in Turgenev's world. Meanwhile, great aspirations and much surface activity persistently occur.

In its concentrated intensity of development the central action in a Turgenev novel is a novellalike "fate-tragedy." "Certain characters are by their nature such that, without ill-will on their part ... they must necessarily, when brought into contact, cause one another the greatest unhappiness."[19] Unknowingly enmeshed in a tragedy of ordinary circumstance, an inspired intruder and an aspiring native fatally attempt to overstep the limits set by culture and milieu. That overstepping constitutes the pathos of the love intrigue. "Love in Turgenev's depictions is least of all physiological passion ... to love another means to wish him well, to believe in his powers, to aspire to draw that person away from the musty atmosphere in which he resides."[20] Given such a love, it is inevitable that the central amorous imbroglio bursts beyond the narrow social reference of an eighteenth-century "domestic drama," although that chamber-sized setting is clearly being emulated.[21] Turgenev does create masterly restorations of delicate drawing-room dramas, of subtle *salon* amours, but they are tellingly enriched by the constant symbolic presence of cultural and political analogues. "The philosophic purity at which Bazarov aims, the political millenium which Nezhdanov and his friends seek to attain, are phantom mistresses which resemble in many respects the idealized flesh-and-blood young women of the society novels."[22] In this regard, Bazarov's femme fatale, Anna Sergeyevna Odintsova, may be admired as a classic specimen of Turgenevan "typified" portraiture.

Odintsova is very much herself, a porcelain-cold creature whose normal sangfroid permits her to arrange, seemingly without calculation, all aspects of life in a convenient, gentlewomanly decor. Yet Anna Sergeyevna is also a great deal more than "herself"; she is a symbolic entity as well as a vivid personage. One of the cruelest ironies in *Fathers and Sons* is that blow of fate whereby Bazarov, the self-styled radical empiricist, falls in love with his "perfect match." Just as her surname is suggestive of the words *odin* and *edinets*, so Odintsova's natural bearing betrays the primacy of "number one"; her constitution is that of the proud independent, the instinctive solitary. What finally aborts all hope of romance, as Odintsova herself recognizes and lectures about, is the deadening likeness between Bazarov's "ideologized" self and her given nature. Bazarov fancies himself the total experimentalist, the completely dispassionate and detached "scientistic" mind; such is the mental construct Bazarov imposes upon his flammable nature. But Odintsova is, among other things and above all else, the human embodiment of "scientism" as a mode of being. For a principled antiromantic like Bazarov, Odintsova is the creature of his dreams. Tragically, for that very reason, she is inaccessible to love.

Odintsova exemplifies but one superb instance of Turgenevan typification. At its best, this is a mode of characterization which keeps in perfect equilibrium the tension between the dramatic and the ideational values of the represented representative figure. It is the only mode of characterization adequate to Turgenev's central intent, as described by L. V. Pumpyansky—to write "a *personalist* novel about cultural problems" that concentrates on the particular, symptomatic fates of those types found among the articulate bearers of culture in a provincial society.[23] Having said that, let us return to our original question. Why was Turgenev impelled to typify character in just this way? Or, to put it in another way, for what conceivable reasons was the Turgenevan novel of apprenticeship so different in core fable and in characterization from the European models?

We have already observed that the central action in a Turgenev novel is novellalike. What this implies is that the fiction is deliberately plotted to concentrate on one central conflict which, in turn, illuminates the inherent disposition of an already fully developed character.[24] In the Turgenevan novel, unlike the *Bildungsroman*, character does not develop; it is tested in the crucible of event. I believe that Turgenev, as a provincial realist, did not share the operational presuppositions about the process of life-apprenticeship that lay behind the great European sagas about the Young Man from the Provinces. The chief difference is that in Turgenev's works one does not find a provincial who enters life's school with a blank dossier. Turgenev's provincials come into the school of experience burdened with much baggage. Each one carries something along, be it a particular set of inflexible mores, a systematic ideology, or a culture-specific dream. In fact, what Turgenev's characterizations strongly suggest is that it is precisely the nature of a provincial to stand before the world with a prematurely polished identity. (Writing in the 1880s, Paul Bourget was startled to note how often the Russian novel tended to be "an epic of disquietude, the sad history of an 'enthusiast' out of his orbit.")[25] In the eyes of a cosmopolitan, a provincial may seem to lack character. But that is not his problem. If anything, the provincial is apt to be oversupplied with a defensive sense of self-definition. The life-apprenticeship of such a figure is likely to occur within a relatively brief span of time, thanks to some peculiarly efficient and violent blow of fate. Such, at any rate, was the tale Turgenev told and retold in his novels.

Like other novels of apprenticeship, Turgenev's must also devote the heart of their narrative to a trauma of "realization," to the problem of "character." For this reason, they have often been labeled "novels of character." But such a term has often led to misunderstanding and, sometimes, to downright disappointment. Turgenev's writing often irritates students and teachers whose critical bias is for "dynamic" as opposed to "static" conceptualizations of character. But what Turgenev does to and with his characters can be described in terms outside that dichotomy. Some may find illuminating, as I do, J. A. Ward's description of the prevailing relationship between plot and character typical of Henry James's works.[26]

> When James composes a novel he is not so much interested in drama-tizing what will happen to the protagonist as he is in dramatizing who the protagonist is. . . . James seeks not primarily to imitate an action . . . *but to discover an action that is an analogue of an idea.* The main function of the action in much of James's fiction is to confront the protagonist with knowledge of himself and of his situation, neither of which has essentially changed from the start.

Ward asks us to designate this type of composition "the novel of relations," being a novel in which psychological and characterological causation and sequence are less important than perceived analogies and contrasts with and among other life postures. The fully developed idea of such a novel often crystallizes in the form of an illustrative scene or an archetypal portrait of cultural relations as embodied in an apprentice figure confronting an inevitable initiation; such novels neither require nor respect the narrative form of the picaresque education, the complicated yarn of gradual evolution and maturation. Although the term has not been in currency very long, it would seem legitimate, and perhaps enlightening, to regard Turgenev as a pioneer experimenter in "the novel of relations." Certainly that particular compositional strategy was not an American innovation alone. The innovative and idiosyncratic form of the Turgenevan novel helped a good many provincial writers discover how best to narrate life as it took shape for the best and brightest of their compatriots.

The Clement Vision

Ivan Turgenev, we have emphasized, wrote curious novellalike novels that yet managed to imply an epic-sized cultural confrontation. The powerful precipitating agency behind this narrative legerdemain seemed to be the author's distinctive technique of "typifying" character. It was a technique tailored to fit both the ideational and the idiosyncratic dimensions of the provincial figure's self-image. Turgenev further devised a formulaic story, a most particular fable of intrusion and rebuff that, to his satisfaction, articulated a realistic model of how a provincial consciousness was likely to undergo the process of apprenticeship to life at large. There are many ways to describe such a novelistic form. Some seem too vague or misleading, like "the international novel" or "the novel of character." Others are perhaps more precise, but unwieldy, like "the personalist novel about cultural problems." It is symptomatic of modern criticism's neglect or apathy toward Turgenev that there is no generally accepted generic term which accounts for the innovative Turgenevan novel. That does not alter the fact that Ivan Turgenev created a distinctive novelistic form. Turgenev was, in fact, writing a uniquely poetic, subtly symbolic "chamber novel"; he created condensed domestic dramas that were simultaneously dramatic analogues of larger-scale cultural confrontations. Put differently, Ivan Turgenev welded together the narrative form and the dramatic strategy of "the novel of relations." In this, he was emulated by William Dean Howells and Henry James—two other provincial realists especially fond of fables of apprenticeship. The connection was hardly accidental. With Turgenev's formal precedents firmly in mind, the early novels of Henry James begin to look like "novels of apprenticeship" in more ways than one. Ivan Turgenev had revolutionized the European *Bildungsroman* to portray the special dignity and intensity of provincial initiations into the lessons of experience.

CHAPTER SIX

Novels of Apprenticeship (1875-1881)

The plum-colored New York Edition of 1909 was expressly designed to display all triumphantly the classic arrangement of Henry James's finest and best nurtured products. A staggering labor of craftsmanship went into the conception of this final gathering of Jamesian gleanings. In his revisions of texts, James was touching up the slightly dulled surfaces of his proudest works. And in his Prefaces, he was weaving a huge and intricate framework which would contain and complement the successive harvests of his creative years. Henry James expended every effort to ensure that his cornucopia was as highly polished as its contents.

By now, it is well known that the mature James skillfully highlighted the precocity of his own youthful genius and that he consigned his baggy monster of a first novel to oblivion while claiming *Roderick Hudson* as "my first attempt at a novel, a long fiction with a 'complicated' subject."[1] What is less generally recognized is that James's description of what a complicated subject should be leads into a discussion of the "novel of relations" without any explicit mention of Ivan Turgenev.

> the painter's subject consist[s] ever, obviously of the related state, to each other, of certain figures and things. To exhibit these relations, once they have been recognized, is to "treat" his idea. ... Really, universally, relations stop nowhere, and the exquisite problem of the artist is eternally but to draw, by a geometry of his own, the circle within which they shall happily *appear* to do so. (5)

The Clement Vision

In the Preface to *Roderick Hudson*, the only literary ancestor invoked
is the great Balzac. Balzac is wheeled forward as the towering,
all-humbling standard of realistic representation, yet his massive
presence, once called forth, seems comically out of place. The young
James is ostensibly berated for not having "done" Northampton solidly
à la Balzac; but this tribute is followed by some turn-about phrasing.
James's 1875 version of Northampton can be considered a "pathetic
evocation" *only* "if intensity in such a connection, had been indeed to
be looked for." But, given his original plan for the projection "at the
outset, of some more or less vivid antithesis to a state of civilization
providing for 'art,' " James finally admits to feeling "no drawback in
this scantness, but a complete, an exquisite little adequacy." (8) In
short, the fable itself called for a "relational" and not a "representational" Northampton. Stripped of its dubious modesty, James's Preface
is really claiming that his early novel would have been exquisite art had
it even better been able "to give all the sense, in a word, without all the
substance or all the surface." (14) In other words, *Roderick Hudson*,
good as it is, was the sort of novel that needed to be fewer parts Balzac
and more parts Turgenev.

We can be certain, however, that in the writing of his first
accomplished novel James was studiously mindful of Turgenev's
precedent. For one thing, the initial stages of *Roderick Hudson* and the
final ruminations for James's Turgenev essay of 1874 overlapped. On
the evidence of that one essay, there can be little doubt that the young
James possessed a brilliant intuitive grasp of the basic compositional
ingredients in a Turgenevan novel. Note how shrewd are the terms of
appreciation which James employs to describe what he regards as
Turgenev's "greatest triumph," *On The Eve*.[2]

> The tale is at once a homely chronicle and a miniature epic. The
> scene, the figures, are as present to us as if we saw them ordered and
> moving on a lamp-lit stage; and yet, as we recall it, the drama seems
> all pervaded and coloured by the light of the moral world. . . . There
> is nothing finer in all Turgénieff than the whole matter of
> Bersenieff's and Schubin's relation to Hélène. They, too, in their
> vivid reality, have a symbolic value . . . and if we wonder how it is
> that from half a dozen figures we get such a sense of the world's
> presence and complexity, we perceive the great sagacity of the
> choice of types.

From this it becomes clear that the ideal of a novelist's exquisite

Novels of Apprenticeship (1875-1881)

geometry of relations, so dramatically proclaimed in the 1909 preface, had been uncovered as early as 1874. Before composing *Roderick Hudson*, Henry James already had a sophisticated comprehension of the interplay of elements within a Turgenevan novel of relations. The young American had divined the mystery of typification that made possible the transmuting of homely chronicles into miniature epics, of closet dramas into cultural parables.

The Russian leanings in *Roderick Hudson* did not long remain a trade secret. By 1879, for instance, W.E. Henley was grumpily noting:[3]

> To say that it is strongly suggestive of an admiring acquaintance with Ivan Tourguénieff is as much as to say that it is tolerably unhappy throughout, and that its ending is miserable indeed. Tourguénieff loves to treat of wasted lives. . . . Mr. James is not averse from practising the study of the same section of social pathology.

Allowing for the inaccuracies of a first impression and for a temperament given to gruff overstatement, Henley's observation is still of service. The impact of Turgenev on the early Jamesian novels is somehow harsher than his impact on the Jamesian tales of initiation. In the briefer tales we could detect the guiding presence of Turgenev by engaging in "situational analysis." Typically, the young American's tales of initiation would differ from the Russian model by adapting a parallel predicament so as to emerge with a reversal of circumstances in the denouement. Again and again the American recast the Russian's initiation scenes in order to permit a greater role for the voluntary principle. James seemed to find it important not to be so dismal as to suggest that the iron rule of circumstance, without consulting free will, was responsible for tripping and bruising the uninitiated.

But the early James "novels of apprenticeship" are far more dismal. These narratives portray human woes that seem inevitable as well as irremediable. Suddenly we find genuinely tragic figures in a Jamesian story. Christina Light, even with the best will in the world, is crushed by the weight of circumstances. Perhaps the fuller context, the specific *realia* required to fill in the longer frame of a novel of apprenticeship tipped James's imagination in the direction of circumstantial tragedy. Whatever the reason, there is a new, mature acceptance of Turgenev's full-sighted view of contingent forces. The temptation to imagine variations and reversals of Turgenevan fables of experience seems to vanish.

Those researchers most aware of James's close acquaintance with Turgenev have sensed a number of familiar Russian faces in the American's novels. Roderick Hudson, for instance, is reputed to be cut whole-cloth from the pattern set by James's 1874 description of Rudin:—"one of those fatally complex natures who cost their friends so many pleasures and pains; who might, and yet, evidently, might not, do great things; natures strong in impulse, in talk, in responsive emotion, but weak in will, in action, in the power to feel and do singly."[4] Not surprisingly, it has become a rather common practice to regard most personages in the early James novels as outright borrowings or composites from Turgenev. To single out Roderick again, he has been said to combine Turgenev's "moral failure" type with his "artistic temperament" type, based on Shubin the sculptor. This approach vaguely confirms the likelihood of a characterological borrowing while easily degenerating into even more vague chatter about the comparative natures of imagined beings. The alleged borrowings seem valid enough, but the certifying materials seem to present a flimsy, impressionistic case.

What has been assumed is that James was patterning his characters on "representational" types of human personality that could be found in Turgenev. But James was as much (and probably more) interested in the 'relational" value Turgenev accorded his representative types. In practice, the dramatically rendered personality of Roderick Hudson is less Rudin-like than is his nondramatic, relational identity within the total fiction's symbolic action. Perhaps the felt hand of Turgenev can best be exposed to view by keeping close watch on how the young James "typifies" rather than "characterizes" his people. As an experiment in clarifying Turgenev's influence on the apprentice novels of Henry James, I shall attempt first to measure the relational value of character to character and of character to total fictive event in *Rudin* and *Roderick Hudson*. Ultimately I hope to specify how James "borrows" Turgenevan characters by looking for similar typifications embedded in analogous fables.

Rudin and *Roderick Hudson* are both novelistic portraits of a young artist; each is a narrative of apprenticeship which relates the rapid and circumstantial rise to fame and the circumstantial and even more rapid disintegration of what had promised, at least among provincial admirers, to be an inspirational figure. And yet, how disparate seem the gifts of the central figures! James's young American sculptor can honestly present himself as a natural wonder; his fate always pursues him in the grand thunderclap manner. Set apart from fellow beings by his vaulting ambition and volatile temperament, he is driven by pride and guilt to bare himself in isolation to the elemental forces of nature. The final combat is uneven, but not inglorious. "He had fallen from a great height, but he was singularly little disfigured."[5] Such an exit is barely short of an apotheosis. By contrast, Turgenev's hero can only be said to talk a good game. Rudin is a gifted rhetorician whose given nature forces him to enact the complex role of an innocent Tartuffe—he is an artist of expressiveness whose virtuosity deceptively inspirits himself and others toward unrealizable projects. Rudin's fate overtakes him in the pathetic fly-swatter manner. In Turgenev's "second epilogue" added in 1860, a feeble Rudin incongruously mans the Paris barricades of 1848, holding a red banner in one hand and a "crooked and blunt" saber in the other. Fired at, he topples "like a sack" crumpling at someone's feet. The fleeing *communards* quickly note that "the Pole" has just been killed. In an ironically suitable epitaph to a hero who has made a career of being a displaced person, Turgenev concludes, "That *Polonais* was ... Dmitry Rudin." Such an exit is little short of farcical. The plain facts of the two careers would scarcely seem to legitimate any comparison whatsoever.

And yet, the pathos of Rudin and the heroics of Roderick are forced to keep close company with one another by the qualifying strength of each author's full context. For two heroes with such different exits, Rudin and Roderick make remarkably similar stage entrances. In fact, that initial likeness is never wholly outlived, despite contrary appearances. What F. R. Leavis asserts is a central concern of *Roderick Hudson*—"to explore the nature of genius ... and a questioning of the relation of creative power to the 'artistic temperament' "—is a focus in *Rudin*, too.[6] For in each novel we are following the tragicomic narrative of the life-apprenticeship of provincial "geniuses." Despite his grander proportions and larger presence, Roderick, like Rudin, "is not a hero, but a comic figure, only one who solicits not satire, but a protective, empathic humor."[7] We are dealing, then, with the tragicomedy of what passes for romantic genius in a provincial culture. But how do we judge what is pitiful and what is grand about these putative geniuses? In *Rudin*, the standard is clear. The true worth of a man is measured by asking some reliable judge (notably Lezhniov), "But how did he speak?" In *Rudin*, gestures typify more accurately than event or even accomplishment, since one's natural manner of articulation is perceived as a sincere pledge of intent. Testing this criterion, we are free to ask of each of our geniuses what his style of self-expression basically typifies.

Of Rudin it should first be noted that his basic style of life, due to circumstances beyond control, is to act as a substitute hero. Although the main character, he has to force himself on our attention as the last-minute replacement for a certain baron who had written an article on political economy "from the aspect of language" and was reputed to "gush Hegel." It is Turgenev's design to deflate systematically all high expectations in the reader prior to the delayed and awkward entrance of his leading man. Just before Rudin intrudes, we are gathered in the country salon of an aging and bachelor-hungry Moscow lioness awaiting the dubious pleasure of a second-string inspirationalist discourse on social realities, all to be served up with philosophical tongue. And when our true hero enters, his stage presence, while attractive, is not exactly commanding. Rather stooped, and with a watery gleam in his darting eyes, "the thin tone of Rudin's voice did not correspond at all to his physical stature and broad chest." (III) Yet, with all these handicaps, the style of the speaker is sufficient to captivate those auditors with the finest imaginations and the purest aspirations. Before the chapter is over, Rudin has trounced the resident cynic, Pigasov, with a passionate defense of the worth of generalities and systems of thought. But Rudin's genius for "the music of eloquence" is indicative of some pathetic imbalances, too.

Rudin's admirable "style" has been well steeped in German Romanticism and long brewed in a Russian postgraduate fellowship, but it is not potion enough to magically transform things Russian. Portrayed positively, it is the style and sensibility of an inspired generalist. "Listening to Rudin, it at first seemed to us that we had finally seized upon it, the general connection, that at last the curtain had been lifted. . . . Nothing remained senseless, accidental: everything was made to bespeak a rational necessity and beauty." (VI) But to possess this talent to the extent of Rudin's ingenuity has harsh human consequences. It means that one's genius puts one in the essentially passive posture of the cosmic rationalizer; one is permanently consigned by the inner eye to see life itself in grand symmetries or else to perceive graceful apologias for whatever is. One of the lesser costs of Rudin's gift is that he is a wretched storyteller. "His descriptions lacked color. He didn't have the capacity to be humorous." (III) In this instance, Rudin cannot relate concretely what it was like being a German student—a small foible, but one which has large ramifications. Rudin has, in fact, no concrete relation whatsoever to the innumerable jagged details that bestrew the path of intellect and the arc of imagination with crippling impediments. His airy tread leaves earth's coarse nature unimpressed, yet he can set askew human nature's delicate adjustments.

Even when most firmly implanted as resident intellectual on the Lasunskaya estate and yielding a project a day, Rudin cannot impinge upon the stubborn Muscovite balance of nature. "In the management of her estate, she clung to the advice of her steward, an elderly one-eyed Ukrainian, a good-natured and shrewd scoundrel. 'The old is fat, the new is thin,' he used to say, placidly smirking and winking his single eye." (VI) The forces of elemental nature may be blind; that makes them no less implacable. But the equilibrium of human nature is far more easily ruffled. And Rudin's analytical rearrangements of human chemistry invariably upset otherwise spontaneous processes. Amidst the chaos of love "he used to skim over all sorts of misunderstandings and tangles like a swallow over a lake." (VI) Clearly, Rudin resists being "grounded." At one point in his lengthy summary, Turgenev's sitting judge in the novel, Lezhniov, describes Rudin's case in cultural and sculptural terms: "a cosmopolite is a nullity, worse than a nullity; apart from nationality there is no art, no truth, no life; nothing can exist. Without a physiognomy there can't even be an idealized face: only banal features are possible without a distinctive physiognomy." (XII) Rudin's style, for better or worse, typifies cosmopolitan idealism taken to a provincial extreme.

Roderick Hudson's typifying style is usually cast in sculptural terms. But as Richard Poirier has effectively stated: "Eloquence of speech . . . is a stylistic symptom in *Roderick Hudson* of personal irresponsibility, of showing, through addiction to language too florid for ordinary sensible discourse, that a character has a deficient sense of his obligation to others and to the complexities of a given situation."[8] Poirier's term for describing such a style is "melodramatic"; for him, it reflects a sensibility that is fixated upon "any stock expression of stylized intensity."[9] For our purpose, it matters what *brand* of stylized intensity is regularly wielded by rude, self-styled geniuses. It is not inconceivable that certain forms of melodramatic expression could be appreciated as catalytic imports within a narrow culture.

As with Rudin, it is important to oversee and overhear attentively the stage entrance of the title hero, since the genius's fundamental style of expression remains constant. Roderick's abrupt manner of nodding rather than bowing, we are told, may indicate he is "scantily versed in the usual social forms"; after he draws attention to the fact that he is "dripping wet" and is fondly reprimanded for doing everything too fast, we witness a carefully posed scene.

> "I know it, I know it!" he cried, passing his hand through his abundant dark hair and making it stand out in a picturesque shock. "I can't be slow if I try. There's something inside of me that drives me. A restless fiend!" (19)

Meanwhile, Roderick's future patron, Rowland Mallet, is in a nearby hammock amusing his hostess's child by pretending to be a cradled baby. He perks up, expresses an amused curiosity to actually see a gentleman with a fiend inside him, but submits to being cradled longer, listening contentedly to Hudson's voice. "It was a soft and not altogether masculine organ, and pitched on this occasion in a somewhat plaintive and pettish key. The young man's mood seemed fretful: he complained of the gnats, of the dust, of a shoe that hurt him." (20) Finally called to meet this harried denizen of Northampton, Rowland is able to take Roderick's measure more closely. "The fault of the young man's whole structure was an excessive want of breadth. . . . The result was an air of insufficient physical substance." (21) Yet, noting how effectively Roderick flourishes his slouched sombrero, "the traditional property of the Virginian or Carolinian of romance," Rowland hopefully observes that the youngster "evidently had a natural relish for brilliant accessories, and appropriated what came to his hand." (22)

Roderick's initial manner is, indeed, florid, sonorous, voluble. Yet to sum him up as "melodramatic" seems unfairly dismissive. The total presentation elicits a more complex response from the beholder. We are likely to feel protective, annoyed, awed, threatened. Roderick is impulsive, yet also a perfectionist; he is fragile and vulnerable, yet disturbingly agile in adopting protective coloration; he is naïve, but cunning, too. Looking over Rowland Mallet's shoulder at Roderick Hudson (and especially after listening to Cousin Cecilia's interjected "typifying" biography), our outlook on the hero is apt to be unsettled. We do not quite know what we are confronting, nor how we should feel about it. James seems to have staged a nervous post-Appomattox sizing-up session between the Cavalier and Yankee temperaments. But this relation promises to be unusually amicable, since the romantic Cavalier is still young enough to be unfallen and the shrewd Yankee is

90

wise enough to make allowances. Once we move beyond first impressions, though, the relation widens to incorporate other values as well. Ultimately, to know Roderick well is to be able to understand what his sculptures typify.

James's novel gradually ushers us through a gallery of Hudson sculpture. In this exhibition, the style of a piece is as allegorical as its explicit content. Before we ever meet Roderick in person, we gaze admiringly upon a bronze statuette of a naked youth drinking from a gourd. In it, we are told, "nothing had been sought to be represented but the perfection of an attitude." (17) The figure is entitled in Greek "Thirst." A bit later, Hudson kindly explicates the symbolism intended. The water-drinker is youth, innocence, curiosity, "a lot of grand things," and the cup is knowledge, pleasure, experience, "anything of that kind." (25) Needless to say, anyone who assumes that such large abstractions are so readily synonymous is both a vague and a blithe spirit. It is typical of Hudson's style of expression that there is a great deal of nebulous romantic attitudinizing beneath a perfectly chiseled neoclassical exterior. In his studio we come across a sculpted memorial to his fallen brother which is "the image of one of the crusaders Roderick had dreamed of in one of the cathedrals he had never seen." (R42) Again and again we see evidence of an impulse to articulate an inchoate provincial reality in classic form. That impulse is not itself classical—it proclaims a high romanticism. It is perfectly consistent with Roderick's paradoxical style to pursue an aboriginal American art "of the biggest conceptions" by embarking for Europe "with a hungry laugh which speedily consigned our National Individuality to perdition." (31)

It is in Europe that Hudson's representative sculptures are exposed for the precious posturings they really are. When the world at large seems to be acclaiming the young American's "Adam" and "Eve" figures, Gloriani, the eloquent spokesman for a realist aesthetic (appropriately a middle-aged man of the world) solemnly warns Roderick against the fatal contest to wrestle Hebraic types into Hellenic shapes.[10] Roderick's retort is both an aesthetic manifesto and a tragicomic cri de coeur. "I care only for the beauty of Type. . . . In future, so far as my things don't rise to that in a living way, you may set them down as failures." (R88) Hudson remains true to this word, and he applies it to all the beautiful things he attempts to appropriate, including the lovely Christina Light. Although his accomplished sculptures do undergo a stylistic evolution, Roderick's own terms for

91

conceiving "style" are fixed. After his notorious "thirst" and his rapidly assimilative digestion have lured him to taste "what is vulgarly called life" in Baden-Baden, Hudson finds himself producing a new sort of sculpture with an atypical, unpretentious title, "A Lady Conversing Affably with a Gentleman." But what can inspirit a Gloriani, for whom "a consummate work is a sort of hotch-potch of the pure and the impure, the graceful and the grotesque," a "report on a real aesthetic adventure," only turns Hudson into a man of moods and discontents. And the more that life refuses to become sculpturesque in Hudson's neoclassical terms, the clearer the connection becomes between his "melodramatic" style of talk and his visionary aesthetic. The fundamental style of our genius, as Rowland Mallet belatedly sees, virtually requires "his never thinking of others save as they figured in his own drama"; our sculptor is a form-fitter with an "extraordinary insensibility to the injurious effects of his eloquence." (R276) Roderick Hudson's style, in art and in life, typifies an eclectic idealism carried to romantic heights. As with Rudin, we are facing the cruel and tragicomic demands issued to life by that prototype of the naïve extremist, the provincial "genius." Beginning with this in-depth resemblance between the heroes, we can start suggesting a true kinship between the novels.

In one particular the early James novel is unmistakably patterned after *Rudin*. It has been said of *Rudin* that it is a novel "whose purpose is to render a verdict on a hero who is understood as an expression of the type of culture that created him."[11] But consider how that verdict is rendered. The reader's normative judgment is prodded by a reliable "reflector" in the cast itself. That reflector, though, is the relational antithesis of the sensibility typified by the genius-hero. From this, a curious tension arises. The reader is led to trust implicitly the judgment uttered by the resident judge, but this does not mean that the reader grants any such implicit trust in the superior worth of the antithetical life-style upheld by that judge. In fact (and here is a very subtle resemblance between the two fictions) the real center of interest, the actual focal point of the reader's imaginative effort, is not what to make of the example of the genius, but how finally to take "in essence and in final effect another man's, his friend's and patron's, view and experience of him."[12] In the end we are virtually instructed how to feel about Rudin and Roderick. But we get no assistance from the printed page in allaying our ambivalent response to the proper lives of the commentator-figures. It can safely be assumed that the young James derived the idea of incorporating a reliable observer within the action from Turgenev's precedent with Lezhniov in *Rudin*.[13] Beyond that, we can watch James's exploitation of some specific relational ironies that complicate our evaluation of Rowland Mallet in some familiarly Turgenevan ways.

Rowland Mallet's structural relationship to Roderick is analogous to Lezhniov's function in "giving the word" on Rudin. But Rowland's "relational" value, what he typifies vis-à-vis the antithetical genius, is a more complex sum than anything figured by Lezhniov. We shall note that elsewhere in Turgenev's fiction there is a relational figure more closely analogous to Rowland's true worth. First, however, Lezhniov's services as a precursor deserve honorable mention. Like Rowland, Lezhniov is assigned the difficult double task of both exposing and condoning the crueler excesses of a romantic genius. To be fair, Lezhniov performs his task with far less sophistication than does Rowland. Initially, he can only abuse; eventually, he can only excuse. Nonetheless, the end result is the recording of a fine balance in each commentator's moral ledger. It is Lezhniov who is cognizant of and warns against the risk of a cruel cheat, a fatal seduction, behind the detached visions of a genius who has no footing in a congenial soil. But it is also Lezhniov who later condones the ramifications of an impractical agitation of society. "Enthusiasm" is ultimately seen as the necessary corrective for a naturally phlegmatic culture. Lezhniov finally comes forward with a valedictory blessing on Rudin's career—"a fine word is also a deed." In sum, Lezhniov articulates a tragicomic appreciation of the meaning and worth of the romantic visionary "genius" similar to that rendered by Rowland Mallet. Yet Lezhniov cannot be cited as the characterological prototype of Mallet. He enters our purview as a colorless sedentary shape wrapped in coarse grey linen and wearing a sleepy smile; he lights up only to express aversion to romantic natures, whom he accuses of always trying to warm themselves at metaphorical fires. We are told that physically he resembles nothing so much as a sack. When we last see him, he is claiming fellowship with Rudin as "one of the last Mohicans" on the frontiers of possibility. But all the while he is vainly pressing upon his odd friend "a nest" of refuge, clearly not comprehending the Rudin who has never "pushed roots into any uncongenial soil, no matter how fertile it might have been." Lezhniov is simply not a clear precursor to Rowland Mallet; he too clearly typifies the *un*passionate pilgrim. At best, he is but an armchair fellow traveler of the genius's visionary company.

There is, though, a *locus classicus* in Turgenev for Henry James's conceptualization of Rowland Mallet's character. We can be guided to it by consulting once again the revealing text of the 1874 essay. To James, nothing seemed finer in all Turgenev than the "symbolic value" of the relation of Berseniev the philosopher and Shubin the sculptor to Yelena, the heroine irresistibly whirled away from them in *On The Eve*. Berseniev in particular struck James as a "poetical figure," one whose history was intensely touching. In giving all the details of his fascination with Berseniev, we can see the familiar figure of Rowland Mallet slowly take on substance.[14]

> He is condemned to inaction, not by his intellectual fastidiousness, but by a conscious, intelligent, intellectual mediocrity, by the dogged loyalty of his judgment. . . . If [others] are born to suffering, they are also born to rapture. They stand at the open door of passion, and they can sometimes forget. But poor Berseniev, wherever he turns, meets conscience with uplifted finger, saying to him that though Homer may sometimes nod, the sane man never misreasons and the wise man assents to no mood that is not a working mood . . . and when he finds that his love is vain he translates it into friendship with a patient zeal capable almost of convincing his own soul that it is not a renunciation, but a consummation.

From this thumbnail sketch of Turgenev's "morally and physically tidy," "conscientiously moderate enthusiast" of knowledge, we can surely point directly to James's "awkward mixture of strong moral impulse and restless aesthetic curiosity" in Rowland Mallet. Both characters embody an analogous dilemma of provincial consciousness. They are aesthetes whose instincts have been debilitated by an inherited cultural mantle that acts as a yoke. Rowland Mallet labors under a residual Puritanism, while Andrei Berseniev toils within a pedantic *Naturphilosophie*; in each case, the legacy of the provincial upbringing is incapacitating. Each man houses simultaneously and paradoxically a sponsoring imagination and an inner check. Berseniev and Mallet can conceive of raptures that the scruples of sober reason will not permit them. In both, an ethically complex temptation arises from a pained awareness of their fated inner timidity: the temptation to sponsor actively or foster passively an experimental substitute gratification.

Berseniev does, for instance, precipitate the fatal involvement of an aspiring heroine and an inspiring intruder by insisting that the extraordinary individuals meet one another. Later, when the risky conjunction is well under way, he consciously steps aside and acts as a willing intermediary in the affair. As a result, we find ourselves uneasily asking how much culpability to attach to the observer and abettor of so patently romantic a scheme. For Yelena's sake, we regret bitterly the lacks in the "safer" Berseniev. We sense that her whole fatally wasteful involvement with Insarov, her whole sad apprenticeship, has been a tragedy by default.

A similarly insoluble calculus of responsibility is explicitly posed before the reader by Henry James in *Roderick Hudson*. The problem is set because Rowland is deliberately conceived as both a Lezhniov-like witness-judge and a Berseniev-like observer-abettor. In fact, the unrevised 1876 edition of *Roderick Hudson* offers plain proof that Henry James intended the reader to consider how morally implicated is Rowland's posture. Early in the novel we confront a dramatic scene which is a tiny paradigm of the whole fiction's moral action. In this scene Roderick is the chief actor, but Rowland Mallet is covertly our true center of interest.

> He strode across the room, seized a mallet that lay at hand, and before Rowland could interfere, in the interest of art if not of morals, dealt a merciless blow upon Mr. Striker's skull. . . . Rowland relished neither the destruction of the image nor his companion's expression in working it, but as he was about to express his displeasure the door opened and gave passage to a fresh-looking girl. . . . Meeting the heap of shattered clay and the mallet in Roderick's hand, she gave a cry of horror. . . . She seemed not to understand the young man's allegory, but none the less to feel that it pointed to some great purpose, which yet must be an evil one from its being expressed in such a lawless fashion, and to perceive that Rowland was in some way accountable for it. (35-36)

Having ourselves witnessed this outburst, it is difficult not to have some inkling of the young James's allegory: whoever is responsible for placing a "mallet" in the hands of a romantic genius has offered wide scope for an instrument equally creative or destructive, enabling or disabling—and some account ought to be rendered for the consequences. The mature James, no doubt embarrassed by the unsubtle object-lesson wielded in this scene, took away the "mallet" and replaced it with a "hammer." Even so, the context remains pointed enough. Before Roderick's ethically and aesthetically destructive gesture of liberation is enacted, we have learned that his patron entertains some bold doctrines himself. Rowland has read in a book that genius is a kind of safe somnambulism; he seems impressed that "the artist performs great feats in a dream. We must not wake him up, lest he should lose his balance." (24) After we have begun to glimpse some of the possible effects of such patronage, Cousin Cecilia extracts from Rowland the tacit acknowledgment that in assuming custody over a provincial prodigy, he is also assuming the imposition of a further responsibility to guarantee "not only the development of the artist, but the security of the man." (45) From this moment forward, the reader has to be drawn into the higher mathematics of moral accounting.

Given Rowland's own divided and self-canceling instincts, there is always the chance that his foster-parenthood to genius will overindulge his puritanical or his permissive leanings and thereby fail. And when Roderick Hudson's beautiful frame is finally carted before us on its rude bier, it is inevitable that some moral abacuses start clacking away. We can, if we wish, blame Hudson's ruin on Christina Light's cruel radiance; we can envisage an explorer of beauty parching on an inhospitable terrain. But we should also recall that Roderick's fatal self-exile from everything human does not occur until Rowland ceases being an imaginative sponsor and begins spelling out the remorseless egotism of genius in its quest for pure beauty. Finally, we can fault Hudson's own melodramatic nature. Whatever we do, the calculus is complicated. What is clear is that Rowland Mallet is both a greater and a lesser figure than the straightforward Turgenevan judge-advocate, Lezhniov. Mallet stands somehow in complicity with the tragicomic extinction of romantic genius; he is subtly guilty before a Rudin-like Roderick. This "relational value" of the sponsor figure may be considered Rowland's Berseniev-like aspect. Equally Turgenevan, however, is the "symbolic value" of the relation of Roderick and Rowland to Christina Light. As in *On The Eve*, an intellectual male and an aesthetic male, a philosopher and a sculptor, are subtly indicted for cruelly failing a truly tragic heroine.

Christina Light develops before our eyes; she grows from a Turgenevan "natural girl" into a mature Turgenevan heroine. In her later Jamesian reincarnation as the Princess Casamassima, she figures as a coldly calculating "capricciosa"; but in *Roderick Hudson*, despite all the false appearances and theatrical artifices amidst which she lives, Christina Light remains until her final defeat a spontaneous improvisatrice. Her given nature, in its unvanquished purity, is both protean and virginal, both sophisticated and vicarious: "the vivacity and spontaneity of her character gave her really a starting-point in experience, so that the many-coloured flowers of fiction that blossomed in her talk were perversions of fact only if one couldn't take them for sincerities of spirit." (R185) She belongs by birthright in the company of Asya and Daisy Miller; she is, as the veteran social commentator, Madame Grandoni, observes, a most interesting mixture of passions "and that, whatever she is, she's neither stupid nor mean, and, possibly, by a miracle, not even false." (R117) Her sort of beauty beggars precise description; but in the aesthetic debate that whirls around Roderick Hudson, she could be considered Gloriani's girl. For Gloriani's undoctrinaire aesthetic offers us the only approach to a just appreciation of Christina Light. "It is a waste of wit to nurse metaphysical distinctions and a sadly meagre entertainment to caress imaginary lines . . . the thing to aim at is the expressive and the way to reach it is by ingenuity." (R83) Only Gloriani's eye is shifting and receptive enough to value a true ingenue. The others in James's cast give Christina a once over and try to encompass her or appropriate her into fixed formulas. It is not only the crass social climber, Mrs. Light, who insists on dragging the "poor original" about the world, passing her off for a stone image of perfection. The story of Christina Light is one constant battle for an appropriate aesthetic and ethical recognition of her complicated natural value.

The relation between Roderick Hudson, the provincial genius, the romantic devotee of classical Type, and Christina Light is a tragicomic affair. The young sculptor's first exclamations and actions upon sighting the "natural" daughter of Mrs. Light typify the root problem of the whole relationship. Roderick is making a rough sketch of the great Juno in the Villa Ludovisi. Henry James makes this particular Juno a symbolic as well as a classical figure. The colossal goddess is sadly resident in a moldy little garden-house and "looks out with blank eyes from that dusky corner which must seem to her the last possible stage‧ of a lapse from Olympus." (77) Nineteenth-century Rome presents itself as an environment which has effectively banished classicism, yet the young American artist is, in all innocence, recreating the glories that once were. When the elegant Christina enters his vision, his enthusiasm leaps to Platonic heights: "In the name of transcendent perfection, who is she?" (87-88) He answers his own question by inserting the facial features of Christina into the sketch of Juno. It is not a happy inspiration. From this moment forward, Roderick Hudson is blind to Christina's true features; he insists on transforming her into a "Junoesque" beauty. This is more than an aesthetic mistake. Looking

97

at Christina Light as if her features have a marble placidity, it is all too easy for Roderick to misread her *ethical* nature as "Junoesque." "In such a face the maidenly custom of averted eyes and ready blushes would have seemed an anomaly; nature had produced it for man's delight and meant that it should surrender itself freely and coldly to admiration." (137) No greater injustice could be perpetrated on the maiden's reputation. The American sculptor is guilty of having carved a graven idol from the vital features of Christina Light. In their immediate relations, it is Roderick who pays the higher price for the misconception—he cannot play hero to a goddess who perceives the comic aspect of her elevation into some pantheon.

The relation between Rowland Mallet, the provincial patron, the rational sponsor of romantic ambitions, and Christina Light is a purely tragic affair. Rowland's complex cast of mind makes him suspicious toward what he would most like to lend some credence. By cultural inheritance, he is deprived of "the simple, sensuous, confident relish of pleasure." (15) He cannot, for instance, yield to a relaxed, sophisticated enjoyment of Rome's mundane charm without nervously fearing a "sort of oppressive reconciliation to the present, the actual, the sensuous." (155) Perhaps, in the special case of Rome, discretion *is* the better part of valor; we respect Rowland's scruples against plunging into a Roman life. But we cannot concede equal merit to his rating of Christina's charms. "It's certainly not the orthodox charm of a marriageable maidenhood, the charm of shrinking innocence and soft docility. . . . Miss Light is nominally an American. But it has taken twenty years of Europe to make her what she is." (170) Rowland Mallet's reasonable expectations bar him from a decent estimate of Christina's moral worth. He simply lacks the imagination to appreciate the rare capacity of some imperfect creatures to wilfully transcend the pressures of contingent circumstance. In brief, Rowland Mallet sells Christina Light short; he cheats her of a proper ethical estimate. His is the chief responsibility for making of her a Turgenevan tragic heroine.

Young Natalya Alekseevna, in her parting dismissal of Rudin, speaks eloquently for all her later sisters in woe. "My God! when I came here, in my mind I was parting forever with my home, with my whole past—and then what? what did I meet here? A man of faint heart." (IX) Natalya's reproach defines what it is that makes Turgenev's heroines tragic: the lack of an eligible hero, an equal partner, amidst one's compatriots. Natalya's response to this plight also sets the sad precedent for her cosufferers. "For anyone the first disillusionment is oppressive; but for a sincere heart that does not wish to deceive itself and is averse to frivolity and exaggeration, it is almost unbearable. . . . Life now stood in darkness before her, and she turned her back on the light." (XI) The true heroine is one of life's irreconcilables; the only path left is renunciation, whatever its perverse turns be. When Christina Light falls from her pinnacle of hope, she is permanently scarred. When Roderick Hudson falls from his height of genius, he is not disfigured. The fall of the enthusiast is tragicomic; but the defeat of the heroine is tragic, for she has not even tasted the palliative of rapture. Rudin's fate had its consolations; Natalya's is inconsolable. So it goes with Roderick and Christina—with one additional complication: the influence of Rowland Mallet. Rowland shares complicity in both fates. Relative to Roderick, he is a Berseniev; relative to Christina, he is a Rudin.

No one seems to have noticed how seriously Christina Light looks to Rowland Mallet for affection and practical sustenance in her struggle against a prearranged fate. From the moment she recognizes his claim as a connoisseur of beauty, she urgently solicits his considered opinion of her. It is more than a matter of seeking approval. It is for Rowland, not Roderick, that she breaks the custom of the country by walking the length of an immense room before five hundred guests to choose his company. And it is at her mother's carefully planned debutante ball that Christina corners Rowland and "comes out" for him with the earnest proposal: "If a person wished to do me a favor I would say to him: 'I beg you, with tears in my eyes, to interest me. Be strong, be positive, be imperious, if you will, only be something.' " (187) Christina's finest performances are all for Rowland's benefit, yet even unearthly Roderick can appreciate her true features better. Probably Roderick's greatest sculpture is his bust of Christina, which James says "without idealization . . . was a representation of ideal beauty." (165) But Rowland is always circumspect; because he is "not fond of exploding into superlatives" he contents himself with suggesting a few alterations. This scene is indicative of Rowland's scrupulously con-strained admiration of life as well as of art, a constraint which blinds him to the finest possible forms that common clay can assume. There is no more damning evidence of Rowland's refined cruelty toward life's beauty than the fact that the defeated, embittered, newly cynical Princess Christina has to announce: "You have seen me at my best. I wish to tell you solemnly I *was* sincere." (450)

Rowland Mallet is a timid aesthete—the man of sensibility as antihero. His consciousness is too complex to be entirely fair.

99

Convinced that life's perfections can never match those attained by art, he is all too willing to see dishonest poses in life-postures that are brave and gracious. Despite the dreadful Cavaliere's dire predictions that Christina's will is chained to the forces of convention, she does break her mercenary engagement to the Prince Casamassima after she has also foresworn her standard "romance" with Roderick. Despite the corrupting demands placed on her life, she has measured up to Rowland's ideal of self-sacrificing, clinging purity as embodied in the provincial Mary Garland. Having renounced both pelf and poetry in life, Christina unsafely casts herself upon Rowland's judgment. The connoisseur, suspecting nothing in her dramatic actions but artful pretense, turns his back on the performance. Christina is left unappreciated in a world that no longer believes in heroic redefinitions of self, liberated from circumstances of nurture. There is no alternative but to be resigned, to renounce all hope of radical alteration. All that is left the defeated heroine is a long lapse into oblivion, or routine, or cynicism. The path of renunciation has many sideroads. It is all the more tragic that the radiant Christina Light becomes so benighted in defeat as to pursue moral backtrails out of a bored self-abandon. A golden girl is broken down into the brazen Princess Casamassima.

In *Roderick Hudson* James managed to tell of two utterly traumatic life-apprenticeships. He related it all indirectly, as it was perceived by an ambiguous figure. The effect of this sophisticated narrative refraction of the brute events was to involve the reader in a complex process of comparative appraisal. The reader's intelligence gropes for a more accurate sense of the "relatedness" of opposed types of sensibility than that conveyed by the internal commentator. All the while, the reader is learning a sympathetic awareness of the comic aspect of judgment in general: verdicts reflect the subtle temperamental adjustments of tragic fact to mundane survival. A high philosophic comedy is present in the Jamesian novel of relations. This is attested by the fact that there is some implicit answer to the challenge: "After such knowledge, what forgiveness?" It is time to ask what knowledge we arrive at in *Roderick Hudson* and how adjustment is possible. For us, it is also appropriate to insist that what James's novel is about is not beyond Turgenev, not deeper than Turgenev, but closely attached, as by a multiveined umbilicus.

The contagious "germ" responsible for Roderick Hudson's tragicomic career had its origin in the opening chapters of Turgenev's *On The Eve*. There, in a riverside conversation accented by symbolic postures, Berseniev and Shubin debate the feasibility of a national form in art very much as Roderick and Rowland do while overlooking the Connecticut River. Especially germane to Hudson's eventual expedition is the following exchange of volleys, initiated by Shubin:

"Just look at the river: it's as if it were beckoning us. The ancient Greeks would have seen a nymph in it. But we aren't Greeks, O nymph! We are thick-skinned Scythians."

"We have our own water-sprites," observed Berseniev.

"Go on with your water-sprites! What's it to me, a sculptor, those offspring of a timid, frigid fantasy, those images born in the closeness of a cabin, in the gloom of winter nights? I need light and space. . . . When, by God, will I get to Italy? . . . I know it! there is no salvation outside Italy."

"You'll travel to Italy," said Berseniev, without turning to him, "and you'll accomplish nothing. You'll only keep flapping your wings and never fly." (II)

It is true that James permits his Hudson to get a bit further aloft than Turgenev's average sensualist, Shubin. But Hudson is launched so high because James imagines his American sculptor as a tragicomic genius like Rudin. Roderick carries Shubin's pseudoclassical aesthetic to Rudin's pitch of romantic inspiration. But a genius for perfect contours means in each case a loss of grip on life itself. James's other sad apprentice, Christina Light, grapples with life in a diverse and tenacious manner, but her very openness to experience makes all the accommodations offered by circumstance too constricting to allow her hopes to thrive. As we have noted, this species of unmated heroine is one of a whole company of spirited spinsters in Turgenev. Even Christina's peculiar path of postapprenticeship renunciation, her cynical and desperate abandon to fortune-making, is prefigured in the amoral career of Turgenev's "legendary princess," Irina, in *Smoke*.[15] To recognize abstract Turgenev models for the two defeated apprentices in *Roderick Hudson* is not to say very much. Relation is all-important, we have claimed. If so, how does *Roderick Hudson* set up a Turgenev-like relation?

Roderick Hudson, the foiled provincial genius, is watched as he twists in those crosswinds of doctrine that made the life of any committed Victorian artist so complicated. The novel can easily be seen as a brooding meditation on the prospects for, even the desirability of, a Victorian aesthetic life. Edward Engelberg, for instance, sees the novel reflecting a struggle to resolve the impasse between "the Romantic's urge for vague and indefinite abstractions" and "the Realist's awareness that such a course is futile"; he defends the "melodrama" of the finale for sounding appropriately "the elegiac note of the last Romantic's death and the survivor's guilt for his victim"; and he cites James's work as "an exemplum of late Victorian ambiguity about Romanticism."[16] There is an unresolved dilemma, a nervously open question lingering after the fictional apprenticeships are over and Mallet's balanced verdict has been heard. In the postapprenticeship world, will the virtues of conscience and consciousness be able to coexist at a level of intensity that will make life both cultured and still worth living? On this score, there is a pervasive melancholy, an unswabbed soreness of regret that James himself confesses as he conducts his whole fictional party away from the earthly paradise of Lake Como and up into the Alpine lucidity of Switzerland.

> It was all consummately romantic; it was the Italy we know from the steel-engravings in old keepsakes and annuals, from the vignettes on music-sheets and the drop-curtains of theatres; an Italy we can never confess ourselves—in spite of our own changes and of all the local perversions and the lost causes, as well the gained—to have ceased to need and believe in. (R296)

Our provincial realist is among the last to dismiss life's felt reliance upon some lingering hint of romance.

In heart-felt essence, Turgenev's *Rudin* is a book extraordinarily like *Roderick Hudson*. It, too, is emotionally impaled on an intense regret over a passing sensibility and an extreme anxiety over whether what remains will suffice for a decent life. We now know that the masterfully executed transition from abuse to excuse of Rudin represents an agonized, mid-stream readjustment by Turgenev of his perspective on a generation of philosophical idealists.[17] To "rehabilitate" Rudin was, implicitly, to relate the painful news that life was becoming devoid of any inspiriting vision whatever. Earlier, in the aftermath of the failed revolutions of 1848, Turgenev had decided that sanity required a stern renunciation of "enthusiasm," but rather soon he was finding it insupportable to espouse merely sane living in Russian circumstances. By 1853 we can uncover frank admissions of Turgenev's inner torment.[18]

Know, then, that without some faith, some deep and firm faith, it's not worth living—it's shameful to live; and realize that he who tells you this is a man who is probably thought to be permeated through and through with irony and scepticism; but lacking an avid love and faith, irony is rubbish—and scepticism is worse than obscenity.

The struggle to imagine some effective coalition of the zealous and the ironic sensibilities came to dominate Turgenev's career as a novelist.

Beginning with *Rudin*, each of Turgenev's "novels of relations" illustrates the dialectical tension separating two antithetical types. The novelist's imagination broods unhappily over the rift in life-styles between Hamlets and Don Quixotes, between men of Intellect and men of Will. Turgenev offers a choice of two spectacles in the most mundane of all possible worlds: the tragicomedy of "genius" and the defeat of reason. To have served a full apprenticeship to life in a Turgenev fiction is to entertain the most minimal expectations of any radical alterations in the outward circumstances of fate. Beyond that, one is free to be indecisive as to how one can best and most fully lead an ineffectual life.

In Turgenev's remarkably even-handed scales of justice, the vision-ary-active and the reflective-passive styles of living are weighted equally. But the relation of one to the other remains hazy. Is their apparently equivalent merit to be read as a sign of reconciliation or of pure impasse? Turgenev's epilogues give a resigned account of the aftermath of catastrophe with a subdued restraint that is eerie; his tone could as easily imply ultimate acceptance or ultimate despair of life. Turgenev, the ex-romantic poet who became a postromantic novelist, is a complex creature of ambiguous moods. As Henri Granjard describes him: "He knew, deep within, that he was a lyric poet who had been born to sing of whatever moved and somersaulted him heart and soul. Yet lyricism, all the same, seemed to him inopportune, even 'inactual' in 'the Gogolian Age of Russian Literature.' "[19] From *Rudin* on, Turgenev's lyrical and logical sides keep rearranging and realigning themselves in fictional patterns that typify a wider cultural relation. Always they find themselves to be antithetical by nature. But through experience they learn to commiserate with one another for their joint alienation from an implacable and virtually immovable reality.

Two companion scenes from *Roderick Hudson* nicely illustrate the technical and temperamental affinities of the young James and the Turgenev just described. These scenes taken together (as they clearly were meant to be) dramatize how "life" conspires to rebuff the sure embrace of romantics and rationalists alike. The first scene takes place in that ancient gladiatorial arena, the Coliseum. Christina Light, still radiant and vivacious, tantalizes Roderick with an offered moment of truth. "I suppose we have not climbed up here under the skies to play propriety." (236) She confronts Hudson with her intuition that he, the visionary, is not himself cast in the heroic mold. Like a true Turgenev heroine, she gives notice that her outreaching imagination will not rest its sights on the hero as given. Instead, Christina's imagination shifts upward to the highest of romantic speculation: "Is that little flower we see outlined against that dark niche, as intently blue as it looks through my veil?" (238) One flower of poesy amid a dark world could restore the heroine's faith; but, for Roderick, it beckons with a fatal temptation. Hudson proposes to stand the challenge: he will scale the ancient ramparts and bear some fresh, celestial gift back to the fair maiden. Christina, who suddenly realizes the inhuman expectations of her vaulting imagination, entreats Roderick to recognize his ordained limits. But Roderick gathers all his thunder and prepares to storm the heights. We are set to witness the awesome spectacle of humans playing at heroics. Suddenly, though, reason personified intervenes. "Rowland had measured with a hard glance the possibility of his sustaining himself and pronounced it absolutely nil. . . . It would be finely done, it would be gallant, it would have a sort of masculine eloquence. . . . But it was not possible!" (239-40) The sensible patron rushes to the rescue and the genius is effectively prevented from undertaking a true ordeal. With a tremor of relief, Roderick offers no resistance. We slump back into reality again and we know full well that the romantic assault did not have a chance of success, yet we feel a keen sense of frustration. We wonder if we quite like trading in romance for reason.

A companion scene presents us with the opposite side of things; yet life still shows itself as the same old coin. We are in the Swiss Alps with Mary Garland and her infatuated admirer, Rowland Mallet, matter-of-factly gathering natural specimens of flowers. Suddenly a heroic prospect opens up. One specimen they had gauged as an easy prize now looks out of reach. Exhilarated, Rowland recalls the Coliseum episode. Gauging everything carefully, Rowland asks Mary to trust him to perform the task. We then watch a successful retrieval accomplished; but the irony is that when "life" permits a daring success, the enterprise is robbed of glamor.

She looked at him and then at the flower; he wondered whether she would shreik and swoon, as Miss Light had done. "I wish it were something better!" she said simply; and she then stood watching him, while he began to clamber. Rowland was not shaped for an acrobat, and his enterprise was difficult; but he kept his wits about him, made the most of narrow footholds and coigns of vantage and at last secured his prize.... It was doubtless not gracefully done, but it was done, and that was all he had proposed to himself.... Mary Garland's eyes did not perhaps quite display the ardent admiration which was formerly conferred by the queen of beauty at a tournament; but they expressed something in which Rowland found his reward. He liked having proof of this to put in his pocket, very much as a "handsome" subscriber to an important cause likes an acknowledgement of his cheque. "Why did you do that?" she asked, gravely.

He hesitated, conscious of the deep desire to answer "Because I love you!" He felt that it was physically possible to say, but that it was not morally possible. He lowered his pitch and answered simply: "Because I wanted to do something for you." (427-48)

Compared to the gestures and rhetoric that punctuated the Coliseum episode, there has been a lowering of pitch, indeed. It is true that we have not been scaling heights on the grandiose scale of the earlier venture, but risk, even heroic risk, has been involved. In this scene, heroics are performed—but all unwittingly. Success is achieved by minimizing the true scale, by taking things step by step and always being reasonable, circumspect, and self-centered. Life being difficult underfoot, real accomplishment has to be an unglamorous, even calculating business. We ask ourselves if it is worth purchasing glory with regular installments of such small coin.

What finally impresses us about these scenes is that they both record defeats. Visible dramatic success in life is seemingly purchased by selling out one's stock in romance. Whether one succeeds or not, one loses. "Life" simply will not yield full gratification to headstrong idealist "geniuses" or to systematically ironical skeptics. The circumstantial fate meted out to both life-styles is pathetic, perhaps tragic. Turgenev and James both pictured life as offering equal resistance to the shapes imposed upon it by visionaries and analysts alike. In their novels, the two provincial realists kept relating the sad apprenticeships of variously typified romantics and realists, flailing for survival amidst the Great Muddle. From a provincial perspective, the relation between Romanticism and Realism was not necessarily one of antipathy. The two outlooks and styles did indeed remain antithetical; however there was room for empathy in their mutual inability to encompass, let alone

105

formulate, life itself. In Turgenev and James, all apprentices find that the practical business of living immerses them in a constricting tide of mundane circumstance. In the bitter end, the only saving recourse is the human imagination which realizes and affirms, with dialectical wisdom, that "really, universally, relations stop nowhere."

Henry James finally posted a public notification of private indebtedness to Ivan Turgenev in his 1909 Preface to *The Portrait of a Lady*. This official accounting was not itself lacking in artfulness. The admissions it makes were strategically timed within the entire narrative of the Prefaces, which constitute a self-portait of the master. The debt is tallied only at the moment when its full retirement seemed a sure prospect. Just as Balzac's name was raised only to pay respects to an influence that had largely been superseded, so too, Turgenev's ghost is conjured up on an occasion when James's own substantial achievement could make it seem pallid by comparison. By 1881, the date of the *Lady's* debut, the Jamesian "novel of relations" had fully attained artistic maturity and become incomparable. Up until that time, the "compositional" loans advanced by Turgenev could still be detected. Those amortized loans are the ones acknowledged in the Preface. It was a bit disingenuous of James not to cite the Turgenev precedents earlier in his self-recapitulation. Still, we can deduce the sum of the debt at its highest since Henry James did not falsify the nature of his obligation.

Turgenev is credited with having taught James how to originate a verisimilar "fictive picture" of experience. The crux of the lesson was that an authentic presentation of experience had to go beyond a merely mimetic representation of the perceptible. Turgenev, in James's vivid recreation of him, began his literary pictures with a vision of persons who had solicited his interest.[20]

> He saw them, in that fashion, as *disponibles*, saw them subject to the chances, the complications of existence, and saw them vividly, but then had to find for them the right relations, those that would most bring them out; to imagine, to invent and select and piece together the situations most useful and favourable to the sense of the creatures themselves, the complications they would be most likely to produce and feel.

This account, it should be noted, plants the standard of verisimilitude on the imagination's home ground. It opposes a representational realism based on a selective heightening of what the senses report. It advances instead a "relational realism" based on the human imagination's capacity to generate the dynamic contexts that propel a given character through his life's destiny. Relational realism begins with "the intensity of suggestion that may reside in the stray figure, the unattached character, the image *en disponibilité*."[21] In other words, it begins by seriously entertaining a *romantic* projection of the protagonist, by imagining the fullest potential of the personage's inherent nature disconnected and liberated from experience. The embryonic character in a novel of relations is, like Isabel Archer, a strangely vivid individual "not confined by the conditions, not engaged in the tangle, to which we look for much of the impress that constitutes an identity."[22] But the mature character in the same kind of novel is that romantic figure as imagined amidst an experience *not* "exempt from the conditions that we usually know to attach to it and, if we so wish to put the matter, drag upon it, and operating in . . . the inconvenience of a *related*, a measurable state, a state subject to all our vulgar communities."[23] Thus, a fictive picture of experience that honors the standard of relational realism will naturally take the narrative shape of a fable of initiation. The early Henry James, following Turgenev, imagines romantic apprentices, figures of fable, dramatically enmeshed in an ever-entangling narrative of mundane relations. Ivan Turgenev taught Henry James how to conceptualize a "novel of relations." That much can be deduced from the public record.

Henry James had plenty of opportunity to understudy the staging of a Turgenevan subject well in advance of writing his first apprentice novels. As early as 1874, H. H. Boyesen was publicizing Turgenev's compositional peculiarities: his compilation of elaborate dossiers on *deployable* individuals and his composite technique of characterization.[24] In the period antedating the triumphant canvas of Isabel Archer's *Portrait*, every longer narrative James wrote was visibly impressed by the young American's introduction to Turgenev's art of the novel. This does not mean that each and every narrative was derivative in the same way or to the same extent. Neither does it imply that a novel of relations must fit a Turgenevan mold. It simply asserts that, until *The Portrait of a Lady* established a new departure in the narrative form of a relational novel, James was writing novels of relations that in compositional form or in thematic structure were indebted to Ivan Turgenev.

The complex and largely unacknowledged Turgenevan derivation of *Roderick Hudson* has been our chief exhibit in advancing the Russian's claim as an innovative influence on James and on the novel form in general. There are other exhibits available, too. But the burden of proof now rests more lightly. The obligation to undertake a systematic "relational analysis" of paired texts is not pressing. A method of procedure has been outlined. Previous scholarship has already traced out the most visible patterns of Turgenev resemblances in the early James. And, lastly, the impact of Turgenev on James rapidly decreases as a measurable quantity; it rapidly becomes an effect of shared temperament. By 1881 the deviations from Turgenev seem more noteworthy and seminal to a clear understanding of the Jamesian novel of relations than do the derivations. Even so, the derivative parts can instruct us as they instructed James; in the apprenticeship, they count. A brief survey can reveal how pervasive was the mechanical imprint of Turgenev on the shape of James's earliest fiction. Noting this, we can perhaps better appreciate the likelihood of a permanent temperamental effect. Mustering a vocabulary to discuss that temperamental coincidence of vision will be my last and most difficult assignment.

Turgenev's name is almost never associated with the string of narrative cameos that immediately preceded the sweeping canvas of *The Portrait*. And yet, *The Europeans* (1878), *Confidence* (1879), and *Washington Square* (1880) are *compositionally* more akin to the Turgenevan novelistic form than even the more visibly derivative earlier novels. To be sure, there are no situational or characterological borrowings; but, technically, these are still apprentice work. In abstract structure these narratives hew to the contours of a Turgenevan novel. They, too, are novellalike novels of relations built upon fables of instrusion designed to typify cultural analogues in the guise of domestic intrigues.

Confidence, it must be admitted, is somewhat exceptional. Its plot initiates a dance of antithetical personages, but it proves in the end to be a light-hearted, sociable quadrille. The pairing and unpairing of its couples signals an analogous play of basic temperaments adjusting themselves. But the romantic involvement does not embody a culture-specific clash of mores. *Confidence* operates more on the level of a private exorcism for James than as an exemplary vignette of cultural relations. James seems to be bothered by an uncomfortable similarity between the temperaments of the experimental scientist and the aesthetic connoisseur. He uses *Confidence* to devise a comic scheme that will assign "acutely conscious" specimens to scientists and "finely unconscious" beauties to aesthetes. Scientific detachment is portrayed as settling for a superficial, flirtatious type of involvement while aesthetic contemplation settles down to an improvised adventure with experience. *Confidence* is a *jeu d'esprit*. Under the guise of Turgenev-like antithetical typifications, it probably expresses gamesmanship and sibling rivalry with brother William, the serious scientific experimentalist.

By contrast, *The Europeans* and *Washington Square* represent serious adaptations of form by a gifted apprentice. Both masterfully evoke feelings of pathos and ambiguity in the wake of a Turgenevan "intrusion in the dust." *The Europeans* elicits more ambiguity than pathos; it relates a high comedy of mistaken identity between provincials and cosmopolitans. By and large, the provincials, who reside in an untrammeled environment, are the disciplinarians of the human spirit; the cosmopolitans, who are accustomed to usages and manners, are opportunists of the imagination. James's complex interrelations among straightforward personalities which embody varying intensities of artless Bostonianism and artful Bohemianism provide a fictional experiment in living between two cultures. Several experiments in Anglo-American miscegenation are simultaneously envisaged, permitting the reader to entertain various cultural consequences following from the reception or rebuff of "the Europeans." The cost of either option in terms of the quality of provincial life is opened to speculation. Very much like *Fathers and Sons*, *The Europeans* is a polished problem fiction, "a comparative inquiry, enacted in dramatic and poetic terms, into the criteria of civilization" which offers us "both sides in a comedy of implicit mutual criticism."[25] *The Europeans* is a thoroughly original masterpiece which is also a perfect structural replica of the Turgenevan novel of relations.

Washington Square lacks the tense ambiguity which results when relations between clashing mores are depicted with a moral equanimity. It elicits more pathos than paradox, relating the tragicomic defeat of the timid optimisms of a sequestered and narrow spirit. Catherine Sloper's story is reputedly based on the anecdote constituting the tale of Eugénie Grandet, except that "unity, compactness, intensity result to a degree which is unknown in Balzac."[26] The exceptions make for a considerable difference, however. In *Washington Square*, the father's suppression and the suitor's exploitation of the heroine do not figure so much as illustrations of social structure; rather, they figure more as analogues for different types of parasitic temperament fostered by

provincial pressures to seem "arrived" or "sophisticated." The difference is that James's suppressed heroine is not victimized by a
socioeconomic environment, but by a psychocultural ambiance. The
narrative housing of *Washington Square* was not structured to accommodate a Balzac "type"; but it nicely fits the sparer, more delicate
figure cut by a Turgenevan "typification."

The derivation of the early Jamesian novels of apprenticeship from a
Turgenevan novelistic model appears under many aspects. It can be an
abstract structural relationship, as with *Confidence*. It can combine
formalistic and thematic influences, as in *The Europeans*. Or it can
manifest itself in thematic and even precise "relational" borrowings as
in *Roderick Hudson* or *The American*. In any event, the influence of
Ivan Turgenev casts a very wide and complicated net over that
polymorphous talent, Henry James, Jr. Discriminating and sober
readers can perhaps now agree more readily with the James who said
Turgenev was his idea of a "novelist's novelist." They can perhaps begin
to appreciate what that claim meant to James. Until 1881 Turgenev was
a pervasive influence on the Jamesian art of the novel. Still, one ought
to keep making distinctions—especially since James, even in his most
derivative early novels of relations, was actively experimenting. A true
forecast of James's formal departure into a new kind of relational
narrative is found, oddly enough, in *Roderick Hudson* and *The
American*.

The American, which was virtually written under Turgenev's eye in
Paris, is often regarded as a fledgling novel incubated in part in the
Russian's *Nest of Gentryfolk*.[27] Surely nothing short of conscious
emulation can explain away the coincidence that both novels manage to
sequester a scrupulous heroine in a convent in order to nullify a hero's
presumptuous faith in his natural right to the pursuit of happiness. And
when we know that James was in awe of the "heroic intensity" of the
Russian Liza's "dusky, antique consciousness of sin" within a "tender,
virginal soul," that he respectfully recognized "depths of purpose in the
young girl's deferential sweetness that nothing in the world [could]
overcome," we cannot help but see the essential outlines of the future
Claire de Cintré.[28] Conversely, when we hear the elderly James
remarking that "the very effect most to be invoked" in *The American*
was "that of a generous nature engaged with forces, with difficulties
and dangers, that it but half understands" and that the fiction's real
focus and concern was "not so much on the particular trick played him
as on the interesting face presented by him to any damnable trick," we

might well recall Turgenev's arbitrary theft of Lavretsky's bliss and the hero's remarkably unbitter valedictory to the legatees of his former garden of romance.[29] The Newman-Claire disengagement in *The American* would seem closely modeled on the relational values expressed by the thwarted union of Lavretsky and Liza. In each case, an intruding hero demonstrates in his life-style a presumptuous, ahistorical faith in his exemption from ordinary circumstance—a faith perhaps endemic to provincial cultures. Christopher Newman is, indeed, a titular American; when in pursuit of happiness, he posits that "energy and intuition can arrange anything." Turgenev's Lavretsky also embodies a symptomatic value. He descends from an ancient Russian family that has a long history of being seduced by sentimental attractions for foreign rationalisms. He belongs to the native aristocracy that is culturally disinherited because it is too refined to be "at home" at home. Lavretsky himself is of serf and gentry blood, somewhat artificially conceived as a "son of nature" by a father enamoured of Diderot and company. Turgenev's hero typifies the plight of a whole culture's engrained bastardy. In seeking to liberate himself from a deracinating enslavement to an alien lifestyle, Lavretsky utters the exorcism, "Vanish, past, dark spectre,"—a sentiment which is itself a romantic aspiration of the French Enlightenment! Like Newman, Lavretsky embodies a culture-specific dream of romantic nationalism. Both are romantic heroes in the purely Jamesian sense—they are equally aloft in the balloon of disconnected experience.

In each novel, the hero is presuming an illusory freedom of arrangement in life's affairs. But the heroine whom he finds most engaging is herself bound to traditions he but half understands. Newman, whom we first meet reclining at his ease in the Louvre's *Salon Carré*, a man to whom Catholicism is but a name, is not exactly alert to the rigid sustaining forms of a venerable history. And Lavretsky, an uprooted runaway from European cultural complications, cannot accustom himself to Old Russia's refuge in a stern quietism; he has absented himself too long from the worldly-wise meekness of a life "sunk to the very bottom of the river." Both heroes are romantic upstarts who yearn for the tranquil and refined beauty of existences formed in obedience to an ascetic, venerable decorum. Liza and Claire embody, respectively, the allurements of an Orthodox piety and an orthodox honor. In the end, the romantic ambitions of the outlandish intruder-heroes cannot sweep aside the formal pieties of a fully arrived culture.

Everything said so far serves to reinforce the argument that *The American*, like *Roderick Hudson*, displays evidence of intimate thematic and relational ties to specific Turgenev novels. It is appropriate that this closeness be fully recognized, provided one key distinction is maintained. The same two early James novels which most transparently derive from Turgenev also violate the Turgenevan novelistic form more blatantly than their less derivative companions in the apprenticeship period. It is not a petty matter that *Roderick Hudson* and *The American* run well over one hundred pages longer than their Turgenev analogues. This deviation from the novellalike novelistic structure signifies an important deviation in characterization, too. Yet we already have claimed that James observed Turgenev's mode of typifying character—even to the extent of emulating the same relational values. What, then, constitutes the difference, and what formal consequences ensue?

A long-standing cliché has it that Turgenev's characterizations are those of a psychologist minus psychology. That elliptic remark can still stand if we regard it as referring to a concern for social psychology and a general interest in psychic phenomena, but one coupled with a distaste for minute motivational studies of particularized psyches. As early as 1852, Turgenev was chastising a dramatist for subjecting his audience to the chore of on-stage psychologizing.[30]

> We shall permit ourselves to remark . . . that this unquestionably useful procedure ought to be carried out by an author beforehand. His characters should already be under his full control when he ushers them before us. But it's psychology, we'll be told; all right, but the psychologist ought to disappear into the artist just as the skeleton vanishes from sight under the living, warm flesh to which it offers a firm but invisible support.

On the one hand, Turgenev's bias favors the poetic virtues of condensation and economy of presentation. But it also reflects a primary concern to portray fully conceptualized personages whose expressive style and dramatic actions will be culturally symptomatic. Again, the centrality of typification to Turgenev's purpose, his need to project the culturally paradigmatic gestures of fable, had immediate technical consequences on his mode of characterization.

In a Turgenevan novel of relations, it is most important that the private drama of interpersonal affairs be perceived as indicators of the *res publica*. All interactions are conducted in the language of publicity.

Novels of Apprenticeship (1875-1881)

"An internal personality conflict in Turgenev's novels reveals itself through the juxtaposition of words subordinated to a logical delivery and an externalized portrait of gestures which manifest the natural sentient being of the person."[31] Turgenev's characters, even in their rare internal monologues, think aloud. They think in quotes, with carefully styled postures. They speak in expressive speeches, carefully delineated in stylistic manner and physical mode of address so as to announce the particular public conventions they underwrite. Turgenev's characters do, of course, also have inarticulate feelings. But they feel through the author's graceful third-person summations; and what they feel is often commented upon and linked to more general formulations of behavior supplied by an omniscient narrator.[32] Take, for instance, the scene where Yelena, under coldly glorious Venetian skies, broods over the possibility that Nature's impassive front in her time of travail is a punishment for her spiritual emigration from domestic bonds.

> "My conscience was silent, it is silent now: but is that, after all, any proof of innocence? ...
>
> "And what of the grief of a poor, lonely mother?" she asked herself, and was abashed, and found no reply to her question. She did not know that every man's happiness is founded on another's unhappiness, that even his advantage and comfort require the disadvantage and discomfort of others, as a statue requires a pedestal. (XXXIII)

Obviously, the author is not striving to disguise his ultimate supervision and staging of the scene. Often enough the meeting of a character's sensibility with his resolved fate is accompanied by Turgenev's own *sententiae*. Only rarely does a Turgenevan character seem himself to be defining a truly private, idiosyncratic relation to a fictive event.

Many of the processes just mentioned happen equally often in Jamesian characterizations, too. We have had occasion enough to note the penchant for attaching allusions that typify, for finding the right admixture of symbolic "flattening" to make characters fit into an economical action that displays patterns of culture. It has not been difficult to espy significant postures or to overhear self-typing elocutions in James's early novels of relations. As with Turgenev, there is an evident unconcern about motivational psychology—the reasons for Roderick's self-banishment or for Newman's renunciation of revenge are either explicitly opened to speculation or implicitly buried in the dramatic surface of the narrative. And yet the record of the life-apprenticeship of a Hudson or a Newman is so much more voluminous than any comparable records penned by Turgenev. What makes the difference and fills out the narrative form is the Jamesian additive known now as "point of view." Building upon Turgenev's thematic and relational precedents, the early James was experimenting with techniques to expand a "relational" fable in order to replicate the actual processing and patterning of perceptions in the psyche of a "typified" consciousness. In the early novels, this narrative experiment was not carried out with total aplomb. But successfully, consistently applied, the technique creates the unique formal properties of the mature Jamesian novel of relations—a sub-genre so distinct that it merits separate terminology.

The breakthrough into an inimitable Jamesian novelistic form came with *The Portrait of a Lady*. Isabel Archer herself can, in the abstract, be placed in a line of descent from George Eliot and Ivan Turgenev by way of Gwendolyn Harleth and Yelena Stakhova. In his rhapsodic response to *On The Eve* in 1874, Henry James had declared: [33]

> The story is all in the portrait of the heroine, who is a heroine in the literal sense of the word; a young girl of a will so calmly ardent and intense that she needs nothing but opportunity to become one of the figures about whom admiring legend clusters.... She passes before us toward her mysterious end with the swift, keen movement of a feathered arrow.

It is extraordinary how James's very verbiage suggests the portrait of a heroine with an intense will for freedom who will be given the opportunity to launch into her natural trajectory as if sprung by an Archer! And it is equally remarkable how well James's description of Gwendolyn's story prophesies Isabel's final trajectory: "The universe forc[es] itself with a slow, inexorable pressure into a narrow, complacent, yet after all extremely sensitive mind, and mak[es] it ache with the pain of the process." [34] But the actual portrait of James's lady is not captured in an abstract sketch; it can only be described in the self-traced arc of the heroine's fully perceived experience.

The Portrait of a Lady was something different, for once, as James himself enjoyed recollecting. [35]

> "Place the centre of the subject in the young woman's own consciousness," I said to myself, "and you get as interesting and beautiful a difficulty as you could wish. Stick to *that*—for the

centre; put the heaviest weight into *that* scale, which will be so largely the scale of her relation to herself. Make her only interested enough, at the same time, in the things that are not herself, and this relation needn't fear to be too limited."

In our context, what James had done was to *internalize* or wholly psychologize a Turgenevan novel of relations. This novel was no longer a narrative of relations; it recorded a *relating* of relations. The focus of the fable had been displaced from the exquisite geometry of seemingly closed relations to the dramatic process of relating idiosyncratic resolutions to one's fate. In the *Portrait* we are glimpsing for the first time what Barbara Hardy has called the Jamesian texture of total relevance.[36]

> The phenomenal world never shines innocently in its own right in James, but it is not reduced or schematized out of existence.... James makes the characters self-consciously formulate the symbolic and personal distortion and this has the special dramatic effect of making the visible world especially relevant while indicating its actual undifferentiated status.

In other words, the whole burden of the composition and resolution of an archetypal clash of mores is being shifted from author to protagonist—not in fact, of course, but in the crucial aspect of seeming to be so. The apprentice figure is becoming a rival novelist, fighting for the autonomy of its imagination amidst the pointed plot devised by the author to illustrate the role of fatal circumstances. Instead of hearing Turgenev commentaries or commentators, we actually witness the perceptive play of an internal composer's imagination, a play that is sponsored and encouraged by a sympathetic fellow composer, the novelist. Perhaps the mature Jamesian form of the novel of relations is more aptly called a "relational" or even a "relativist" novel. Certainly the formal apprenticeship to the Turgenevan art of the novel concluded once Isabel Archer's portrait had been fully crafted.

And yet even the mature Jamesian relativist novels of apprenticeship still bear traces of a temperamental affinity with the imagination of Ivan Turgenev. To the extent that a given Jamesian narrative concerns itself with the imaginative possibility of a *post*apprenticeship period, it still echoes one of the primary concerns of the Turgenevan vision of existence. The Russian and the American do share a common sensibility. Their mature art describes not simply a "tragedy of manners," but something beyond tragedy as well. As provincial realists it befitted their function to tell and retell stories about the futility of romantic ambition pathetically outflanked by flocks of mundane contingencies.

Richard Poirier has summarized the drift of the early James novels by describing the final plight of the characters who matter most as "a patience akin to death, in which fineness of impulse loses confidence in its social efficacy."[37] He sees all the early novels, from 1875 to 1881 inclusive, as tragedies of manners in which the author's partisan delight in his own defeated improvisers adds a fond elegiac coda to the inevitable death-knell. But even in the early novels, it is rarely the case that defeat is so wholly an unmixed, unambiguous catastrophe. Cornelia Pulsifer Kelley offered some wise counsel on how to interpret the external impasses that conclude so many Jamesian apprenticeships. "It must not be overlooked, however, that defeated though she is externally, Isabel achieves a moral victory for herself. . . . Isabel, thus, is like Newman in *The American*. Behind it all is the influence of Turgénieff and his use of failure, now thoroughly absorbed by James as a dominating principle."[38] Please note the careful stress on the *relativity* of the protagonist's victory. The reader may not share the sensation or may feel ambivalent about it, but it is there. Whether one calls it triumph or not is a moot point. What matters is that over and beyond the overt "tragedy of manners," James has superimposed a final "comedy of mind."

No one perceived this salvaging admixture of high comedy more eloquently than Constance Rourke, who was also the first to recognize that Henry James had made defeat for the American adventurer a key component in our national portraiture.[39]

In comedy reconcilement with life comes at the point when to the tragic sense only an inalienable difference or dissension with life appears. Recognition is essential for the play of a profound comedy; barriers must be down; perhaps defeat must lie at its base. Yet the outcome in these novels was in a sense the traditional outcome, for triumph was comprised in it; but the sphere had altered from outer circumstance to the realm of the mind and spirit; and triumph was no longer blind and heedless, but achieved by difficult and even desperate effort.

Finally, no one sensed this same salvaging admixture in Ivan Turgenev's melancholy narratives as keenly or as profitably as Henry James, Jr.[40]

Novels of Apprenticeship (1875-1881)

We can welcome experience as it comes, and give it what it demands in exchange for something which it is idle to pause to call much or little so long as it contributes to swell the volume of consciousness. In this there is mingled pain and delight, but over the mysterious mixture there hovers a visible rule, that bids us learn to will and seek to understand. So much as this we seem to decipher between the lines of M. Türgénieff's minutely written chronicle.

CHAPTER SEVEN

What James and Turgenev Knew:
The Clement Vision of Experience

Une fois que la vie personelle égoiste (la seule vivante)—est finie—(et c'est un peu, je crois, votre cas—car cela arrive aux jeunes aussi bien qu'aux vieux) ce n'est plus qu'une question d'adaptation;—si l'on s'arrange tolérablement dans son milieu—c'est tout ce qu'on peut demander.

Ivan Turgenev to Henry James
February 28, 1877

Prolonged exposure to the novels and stories of Henry James or Ivan Turgenev has been known to induce a state of depression in sensitive readers. Quirks of temperament aside, any knowledgeable reader of these two writers must surely accustom himself to the regular spectacle of dashed expectations and overt defeats; willingly or no, one becomes a feeling intimate of "superfluous" heroes and stoical heroines. Paul Bourget, writing of Turgenev alone, stated the general case well: "The customary substance of these narratives is the story of hope aborted." No one, he felt, better seized and rendered the precise moment when an illusion dissipated and a harsher reality imposed itself.[1]

The sharp constriction of human possibility that so invariably awaits in these narratives of life-apprenticeship has led many commentators to commiserate with James and Turgenev for an alleged preoccupation with defeat, loss, and renunciation.[2] To be sure, a whiff of defeatism does emanate from the final pages of these tales of destiny. The world, as represented in the scenes and pictures of James, does rain down fatal blows on the original aspirations of his "free spirits," as Isabel Archer was one of the first to discover. Yet these defeats are, often enough, only ostensible. In addition to the "conscientious realism" which sternly depicts a world destined to thwart romantic aspiration, James also envisages a "conscious realism" of imaginative processes which may subsume the experienced world in a redemptive perception.[3] Even to a postapprenticeship awareness, life can claim precious worth. It is precisely such a capacity for a disabused bewonderment that is also affirmed in the mature world-view of Ivan Turgenev. As I shall argue, it is in the celebration of this perceptual "victory" that posterity can best glimpse the profound temperamental affinity that linked even the late James to the mentor of his youth. It is true that the burden of negativism sometimes attributed to Henry James was once laid squarely on Turgenev's shoulders by James himself. Upon first acquaintance the young James was an appreciative but depressed observer of the Turgenevan world. Later, though, Henry James caught himself in the act of misperception and, to his credit, made generous amends.

Perhaps the most poignant passage in the brief and generally reticent correspondence between Turgenev and James is found in the Russian's opening remarks. In a charming and halting English Turgenev modestly accepted the strictures as well as the praise proclaimed by his new-found American friend:[4]

> I have only to observe, that the pessimism you reproach me—is perhaps—is certainly—an involuntary one.—My "excess of irony," as you call it—does not give me any pleasure—not even the bitter one, of which some people speak.

Turgenev was protesting, but not strenuously, his young admirer's allegation that a "wanton melancholy" pervaded the Russian's particular stagings of the human scene. This shocked awareness of Turgenev's minimal confidence in the power of human volition James did not readily overcome. Not until 1877, after a warm personal relationship had been established, did Henry James begin to perceive something behind or beyond the surface resignation to the rule of depressing circumstance. Suddenly, what seemed characteristic in Turgenev was his especially vivid perception of "the side on which human effort is comical, and helpless, and ineffectual".[5]

> Ivan Turgenev's heroes are never heroes in the literal sense of the word, rather quite the reverse; their function is to be conspicuous as failures, interesting but impotent persons who are losers at the game of life. . . . Their interest, in his hands, comes in a great measure from the fact that they are exquisitely conscious of their shortcomings. . . . His central figure is usually a person in a false position, generally not of his own making, which, according to the peculiar perversity of fate, is only aggravated by his effort to right himself.

Here is the dawning of a new awareness in James. The spectacle of failure, even when it has been precipitated by the perverse machinations of fate, need no longer seem either "wanton" or "melancholy." Henry James was now receptive to the possibility that losers could be interesting. Apparently, the consciousness of someone overtly defeated by cruel circumstance could readily solicit the interest of a keen moral and aesthetic imagination. Above and beyond an overt tragedy of manners, James is beginning to glimpse the potential for a superimposed drama of consciousness. Without the sudden expansion in James's imaginative hospitality toward the many failed and victimized heroes in Turgenev, it seems quite likely that a Christopher Newman or a Hyacinth Robinson might never have been conceived.[6]

James quite rightly continued to insist that Turgenev concerned himself with histories of exquisite failures; yet, in context, these fatalities were not necessarily depressing. As a good reader, James now appreciated how, despite the inevitable manacling of "free spirits," life's prospect could still appear broad; in Turgenev's last paragraphs something continued to be ventured even if pitifully little seemed to be gained. Reading Turgenev today, we can see that whether a given apprenticeship ends with a defiant flaunting of superfluousness (as with Dmitry Rudin) or with an abstemious withdrawal from secular fulfillments (as with Liza), the text itself eloquently implies a lasting empathy for the human venture toward unrealizable visions of felicity. No matter how bleak the defeat that prevails in the end, it is something of an artistic signature in Turgenev and James to leave someone or some word behind to memorialize the romantic aspirations we have seen · expire in the final chapters. Thus, Densher lives on in psychic fealty to his "winged dove," Milly Theale; and even a deflated rhetorician like Rudin receives a valedictory tribute from the spokesman of sanity and stability when Lezhniov proclaims "a fine word is also a deed." In the earliest of Turgenev's novels the impulse is present, albeit on just a syntactic level, to assert the ultimate convertibility of fine words into fine actions. There is some promise that articulation may possess the power to redeem, if not reverse, defeats.

By 1877 Henry James reached a fresh understanding of Turgenev's studies in failed ambition; gradually, he came to perceive how an artist could concentrate on dramas of disillusionment without attaching his authorial voice to an absolute pessimism. Still, the young James was neglectful of one whole dimension of human potential within the ken of Turgenev's comprehension. He did not imagine that Turgenev could imagine the possibility of snatching victory from the jaws of defeat. It took a later, more visionary James to fully appreciate an additional side to Turgenev's mature perspective on the human scene—the possibility of a triumph of perception over predicament, the real prospect of an aesthetic redemption of a banal, amoral reality.

In 1897 a fully mature Henry James agreed to testify once again concerning the private legacy he had inherited from Ivan Turgenev. He did so in a piece intended to proclaim the Russian writer's proper place in *The Library of the World's Best Literature*. The essay he wrote stands as a fair measure of the permanent stature Turgenev had attained in the eyes of a former pupil. James's tribute to Turgenev as "the novelists' novelist" is what now is best remembered, but the testimonial should be consulted in its entirety. With a serene confidence in his own credentials as a judge, James was prepared to speak directly about the unique charm and the peculiar vision of a Turgenev recollected whole.[7]

> It is the beauty (since we must try to formulate) of the finest presentation of the familiar. His vision is of the world of character and feeling, the world of the relations life throws up at every hour and on every spot ... his air is that of the great central region of passion and motive, of the usual, the inevitable, the intimate—the intimate for weal or woe ... what, if we have to specify, is finest in him [is] the effect, for the commonest truth, of an exquisite envelope of poetry.

James succeeds in conveying one central impression amid his formulations and reformulations of the Russian's essence. It is that Turgenev's art performs the wondrous feat of suspending an unrelentingly mundane reality in an "element of poetry." James discovers, in short, a prevailing atmosphere which transforms a disenchanting world into a thing of beauty. This effect is achieved by insisting on a perspective that places "character, character expressed and exposed" at the axis of reality. The reader is ultimately encouraged to regard human experience "realistically," but to understand that all external contingencies are phenomena subject to the shapings and refinements of consciousness. By 1897 Henry James had come to perceive Turgenev as a poetic realist whose aesthetic vision was defined by his special treatment of a special subject. What still kept Turgenev's art unrivaled was "the genial freedom—with its exquisite delicacy—of his approach to this 'innermost' world, the world of our finer consciousness."[8]

To a remarkable extent, Turgenev and James were temperamentally disposed to salvage bliss from the banal; they shared a visionary bias that lent a peculiar emphasis to their practice as realists. In contemporary parlance, their realism tended to be of a "phenomenological" variety. In many instances, through their perfection of technical devices of a narrative point of view, their writing encourages readers to construe reality itself as a relativist phenomenon, being defined solely by the quality of imaginative activity within a given human reflector. And in their most ambitious, most visionary narratives experience itself becomes an aesthetic process, a highly dramatic comedy of mind which progresses from initial bewilderment toward eventual bewonderment. Whatever adjectives might be pinned on to fix the identity of this variety of realism, the central fact is that the narrative deliberately draws attention to the capacity of human perception for deriving felt values from neutral or hurtful circumstances.[9] Such a narrative strategy can be witnessed in a tale singled out by James in 1897 as one of Turgenev's "most striking" and in a Jamesian masterpiece from that same year. The deep affinity between James and Turgenev is probably nowhere better observed than in the coincidence of vision which creates a spiritual bond between the Volodya of *First Love (Pervaya Lyubov')* and James's extraordinary Miss Farange in *What Maisie Knew*.

As narratives, the two tales would surely be included together in any informed selection of the world's finest and most famous renderings of a child's passage into adulthood.[10] They also occupy a distinctive and extreme standing among the fictional experiments of Turgenev and James. Both are radical departures from the customary framework of each author's "international tales"; in them, adultery has displaced Europe (or the cosmopolitan manor house) as the way station through which an uninitiated purist must ritually pass into maturity. As literary anecdotes, both are shaped from unusually raw primary materials; they delve into matters Turgenev and James were normally only too happy to consign, contemptuously, to "the school of Zola." The rotten core of these tales is a seemingly willful psychic and sexual brutalization of mere children. Yet, with customary delicacy and indirection, the potential for a shocking, melodramatic impact gets attenuated as subtler astonishments get woven into the fabric of these narratives. In what is a distinctively Turgenevan manner, the element of surprise for the reader shifts from the arena of action to the puzzleboard of reaction.[11] For, finally, these are tales in which an aesthetic sensibility successfully surmounts both delusions and disillusionment. The true watermark of these narratives is not their skillful unfolding of a child's coming to knowledge, but their eventual epiphany of awareness in which precious worth is discovered to adhere to what would seem the most mundane, antipoetic stuff of life.

The intense lyricism of *First Love* springs from an unpromising source. The "frame" narrative deftly sketches the stale atmosphere of a gentlemanly postmidnight private "smoker." An entertainment is proposed to lift the late night ennui; the married host and his two "not so young" bachelor friends will regale each other with their exploits in "first love." But foggy memories and lives of dull routine take their deadly toll until a certain Vladimir Petrovich modestly concedes that his experience was "not entirely usual." Not being good at "storytelling," he volunteers to recount his experience in a notebook. What follows, *First Love* proper, is the formal written reminiscence of a reticent middle-aged bachelor who has found himself lingering after hours in other people's sedate homes.

The reader suddenly is revisiting (in the past tense) the landscape of a boy's sixteenth summer. It is a landscape which betrays the hand of a master storyteller named Ivan Turgenev. We first learn that young Volodya was living with his indulgent, respectable parents in a suburban Moscow cottage located *protiv Neskuchnogo*; topographically, Volodya is situated "opposite the Neskuchny Park" which, he will soon discover, is invitingly lush and dark. For a young adolescent, it is a precarious location; but there is another sense in which he is living opposite the park. Volodya is also situated, through a verbal omen, in an environment which is "against the not dull"—*skuchnyi* being the Russian adjective for tedious and boring. As Volodya will also discover, the suburban freedom granted him by his permissive parents does not extend any license to break social or cultural proprieties. Yet he is at that "dangerous age" when, despite the storybook flowering of childish and chaste dreams of knighthood, he is suddenly susceptible to "the joyous feelings of effervescent young life." In terms of physical and biological placement, Volodya is uncomfortably situated; he is painfully wedged between powerful constraints and latencies. Meanwhile, in one wing of the summer house he inhabits there is a wallpaper factory where boys of Volodya's age press out gay patterns with the full weight of their fragile bodies. Beautiful designs are being produced, despite abject circumstances of virtual servitude. Thus, in the opening vignette of Volodya's situation we see a precariously sheltered adolescent barely separated, externally or internally, from an efflorescence of organic energy. In the background, we hear the sounds of boys at hard labor, engaged in a rudimentary aesthetic process. The landscape itself forecasts the initiations it contains.

Like so many of Turgenev's narrators, Volodya first enters the scene of an important incident as a hunter. His favorite sport is sniping at crows, birds he hates for being "cautious, predatory, and sly." Initially, the boy's hunting takes the curious form of a private vendetta; he feels morally offended by the elusive and ravenous birds. One evening, while tracking these cunning creatures of appetite, Volodya accidentally encounters the remarkable Princess Zinaida. He catches her in the act of casting explosive gray flowers at the foreheads of some young admirers; quite literally, Zinaida enters the scene with a burst of beauty in the minds of men. Himself astonished, Volodya drops his gun. Later, in the fifth chapter, Zinaida will let fall a book upon first sighting Volodya's physically imposing father. These parallel episodes rather dramatically signal the "real events" occurring within scenes of casual meetings; some readers may object to the obtrusive symbolic gestures Turgenev has planted in these moments. But the "melodrama" points up more than the existence of a love triangle; it makes emphatic the important point that both Volodya and Zinaida are capable of experiencing awkward "off guard" moments. No matter how seemingly opposite one another, Volodya and Zinaida are both innocents abroad in a world of startling erotic force. Each shall have to learn to accommodate mature experience: one by abandoning a simplistic moralism easily disarmed; the other by putting aside a bookish romanticism easily tattered.

In Volodya's reckoning with experience, we can observe a central tension between an ethical and an aesthetic sensibility. Irresistibly attracted by Zinaida's beauty, it is his fate to cross over a symbolic threshold into his first love's native environment. Zinaida's mother and her mode of life repeatedly offend the boy as *neopryatnyi* or *neblagoobraznyi*; unfortunately, the seductive vitality of the young girl has been fostered by just such an "untidy" atmosphere which is decidedly "not in good form." It is in this unnerving milieu that Volodya's shy fastidiousness is put to its first test. While carding wool, Zinaida contrives to bind the boy's hands; she then begins to interrogate her would-be suitor. Her line of questioning is significant. Cautiously, she samples the elasticity of Volodya's moral imagination. "No doubt, you have prejudged me?" she inquires. Next, in the wake of Volodya's bewildered stammerings, she appeals to the adolescent to revert to the experiential honesty of children, who speak their feelings openly. It is soon after this that Volodya fails his first ordeal. When he indirectly lies about his age, Zinaida gently raps his hands. This slight reprimand subtly initiates a major theme in *First Love*: the "blow" of fate which inevitably avenges any human failure to face one's actual experience. During a game of forfeits in the seventh chapter, Volodya's reticence prevents him from whispering his "secret" into Zinaida's ear. In response, she smiles slyly; then, at the first opportunity, she metes out a sharp public blow on his fingers. Throughout Turgenev's tale, there is a steady escalation in the punishments dealt for circumventing the inner truth of experience. In the ninth chapter, the infatuated Doctor Lushin attempts to exorcize Zinaida's charm by covering himself in the protective mantle of cynicism. But when he attempts to dismiss her as a coquette and actress, he goes too far. Penitent, he permits Zinaida to prick his self-righteousness by literally sticking a pin in his hand. The climax of this symbolic sadism is reached in the twenty-first chapter. There, it is Zinaida who is on the receiving end. The whipping administered by Volodya's father strikes immediately after Zinaida voices a hopelessly self-deluding command: *"Vous devez vous séparer de cette [femme]."* The ultimate "blow" in the text is the "stroke" which carries off the father on the very day he pretentiously advises his son to "fear the love of woman . . . that poison." There is, then, a symbolic sequence of escalating reprimands that punctuates Turgenev's text. Whenever moral timidity prompts a conscious evasion of actual experience, the text administers a blow of fate *(udar sud'by)* to demonstrate the inescapable revenge taken by the suppressed natural impulses.

Although *First Love* testifies that the lessons of experience are regularly imparted only through violence and trauma, that is but half the story. The process of initiation also involves an expanding awareness of life's energies that, within Volodya and Zinaida, is an aesthetic revelation. The fall from innocence is couched in a poetry of perception. For instance, Volodya's communion with the "sparrow's night" after his failure to utter his secret is a singularly lovely premonition of his bleak life experience. The ghostly beauty of the remote storm with its mute lightning and temperate flashes corresponds to the eerie calm of the mature bachelor's exile from love's realm. "That silent lightning, those restrained glints of light, seemed to respond to the muted, secret eruptions which flamed up in me also." Likewise, Zinaida's improvised poem in the eleventh chapter is a precocious intimation of her mature fate. This vision of a virgin adrift, borne by a relentless current toward a procession of bacchantes, and her half-voluntary abduction into the woods is a poetic forecast of Zinaida's ambivalent but somnambulistic attraction to the animal magnetism of Volodya's sensual father.

The experience of first love takes on a special texture as Turgenev sculpts its contours. The child's plunge into adult sexuality is captured in lines that emphasize the brutal outrushing of pent-up sado-masochistic impulses, and yet it is also frozen in postures that convey the artist's ultimate equanimity. Volodya's actual "fall" is prefigured comically in his recurrent stumblings onto his knees. Then, in the pivotal twelfth chapter, at Zinaida's whimsical beckoning Volodya suddenly plummets himself down from a conservatory wall; he falls into the dust at her feet, is caressed, and arises only to hand his Princess her umbrella. The entire scene is drenched in a capricious cruelty. But it is also a parodic enactment of a painful quixotic theme: the sudden transformation of chaste courtly lover into the abased servitor of an earthly passion. In one brief moment Volodya is demoted from the rank of knight to that of page of *amour*. Zinaida's fall, her loss of virginity, is similarly painted in mixed colors. The crucial chapter in her life is the fifteenth. On the pretext of illness she has been avoiding company; but one night Volodya inadvertently witnesses his Princess in a paroxysm of frustrated passion. At her window, she wrings her fingers, violently shakes her curls, and finally makes a decisive affirmative nod with her head. Three days later, an unknowing Volodya unwittingly extracts the truth about her agony:

> "Are you still unwell?" I asked her.
> "No, now it's all past," she answered as she plucked a small red rose.
> "I'm a bit tired, but that, too, will pass."
> "And now will you be the same as before?" I asked.
> Zinaida raised the rose to her face—and it looked to me as if the reflection of the bright petals had struck her cheeks.

At the end of this amusing interview, Zinaida offers the red rose to Volodya and it is taken. Volodya's innocent acceptance of the beautiful carnal rose is a charming anticipation of his later conscious reconciliation with errant life in a victory of his aesthetic sense over his moral sensitivity.

Through Volodya's eyes Zinaida has come to image vitality, life itself in all its intensity and contrariety. In a key meditative passage in the ninth chapter, the aggrieved adolescent, "like a beetle pinioned by its leg," keeps circling in body and mind around a favorite spot; despite

127

the keen resentment of his wounding, Volodya is emotionally am-
bushed by "a nameless sensation that included all feelings." Lovingly,
he gives to this rich pansensorium of all vital feelings the name
"Zinaida." For Volodya (and, one suspects, for Turgenev), the vivid
and exuberant alternating currents of Zinaida's nature have come to
exemplify that maelstrom of possibility that experience contains. And,
interestingly, neither Volodya nor Zinaida can withhold admiration for
the boy's father, who, though insufferably callous and cruel at times, is
also the only person who can gracefully ride the horse, Electric. The
torment of first love has brought both Volodya and Zinaida to an
awesome perception of the powerful protean flux of organic forces.
Turgenev's tale interweaves two threads of initiation thereby assuring
that all spectators will finally face up to the full tangle of knotted
desires. *First Love* is designed to make readers come up against life's
virtually criminal erotic vitality. Is there an implicit response to the
burden of such an awareness? In the aftermath of what "first love"
reveals, how might one sanely live? Neither in anger, nor in despair, but
in a mood of alert reconciliation, keeping an outlook for each new
upwelling of unsolicited beauty—such would seem to be the implicit
strategy of the adult narrator of *First Love*.

Volodya is, in the course of his initiation, proffered three modes of
seeing life through. His father, a man of physical strength and strong
impulse, advises: "Belong to yourself: that is the whole art of
life . . . know how to desire, and then you will be free, and you will
command." Dr. Lushin, the self-protective cynic, warns: "No matter
where the wave carries you, it is always bad," so be "capable of getting
out in time, of breaking the net." But the boy's ultimate revelation (the
one that enables him to become the clement-spirited memoirist of his
own entrapment in amoral "first love") recommends neither assault
upon nor recoil from the seductions life contains. Volodya's deepest
illumination occurs at the deathbed of an old hag, a wretched creature
who has grappled all her life with the antipoetic specters of disease and
deprivation. The boy observes with fascination that only after the last
glimmer of *consciousness* had fled from her eyes did the crone lose the
terror of death written upon her countenance. Turgenev's cruel tale of
first love dramatically concludes with a coda which intones, Dylan-
Thomas-like, a reverence for the stark, inhumane vitality of organic
energies; having seen "the last wave by," even the wretched of the
earth "do not go gentle into that good night." In the powerful, even
worshipful, conclusion to *First Love*, Ivan Turgenev is not significantly

distanced from his semiautobiographical narrator. The very telling of the tale has realized a vitalistic aesthetic, a cultivation of appreciative sight for forces gracefully deployed, for motions gracefully executed amidst the fecund and amoral energies at play in life. Turgenev might well have said of his Volodya what Henry James decreed of his Maisie: "To live with all intensity and perplexity and felicity in its terribly mixed little world would thus be the part of my interesting small mortal."[12]

In the 1909 preface to *What Maisie Knew*, James offers what must be a close approximation of his vision of realism. "No themes are so human as those that reflect for us, out of the confusion of life, the close connexion of bliss and bale, of the things that help with the things that hurt, so dangling before us forever that bright, hard medal, of so strange an alloy, one face of which is somebody's right and ease and the other somebody's pain and wrong." (143) Certainly within his novella it is the primary function of Maisie Farange's child's-eye-view to draw the reader's attention to the latent beauties in life's so strangely wrought medal. As James again so well expresses it, "she has the wonderful importance of shedding a light far beyond any reach of her comprehension; of lending poorer persons and things, by the mere fact of their being involved with her and by the special scale she creates for them, a precious element of dignity." (147) Maisie has the shocking innocence that is capable of staring at the colorful interchanges of adult partners much as a child stares at the flowing contours of magic-lantern slides as they pass in rapid succession. Through her magic lens, Sir Claude, her mother's second unfaithful lover, is "dignified" to such an extent that he becomes a virtual typification of James's pleasingly ambiguous medal of life. He is cast in James's recorded image of Turgenev's Rudin; he, too, is "one of those fatally complex natures who cost their friends so many pleasures and pains; who might, and yet, evidently, might not, do great things; natures strong in impulse, in talk, in responsive emotion; but weak in will, in action, in the power to feel and do singly."[13]

Finally, Maisie's "wonder working" emerges in her capacity not merely to accept, but to appreciate lovingly Sir Claude, even after she has divined his incorrigible inconstancy. The true climax of *What Maisie Knew* is not an epistemological breakthrough, for the reader cannot gauge with certainty Maisie's grasp of the adult "plots." Rather, the climax is attained with Maisie's ability to impart a value and a dignity to what she can perceive (however limited that may be) as morally inadequate. Maisie's extraordinary sensitivity enables her confrontation with sordid erotic experience to culminate in an aesthetic epiphany. What Maisie could conceive from experience is more centrally significant than what Maisie either did or could objectively "know." The essential plot of James's novella is the process of maturation whereby Maisie and, in her wake, Sir Claude retrieve something of value from the frequently immoral games that adults play.

In *What Maisie Knew*, James eavesdrops on a gifted child's miraculous transubstantiation of a rank domestic swamp. At first, the reader is treated to the comic perspective of a child's uninhibited game sense as it operates on the raw material of divorce court annals. The uninitiated youngster employs the vocabulary of parlor games to cope with the erratic movements of her parents and their domestic helpers. Her various governesses seem to Maisie to be engaged in "some wild game of 'going round.'" The rules of the game seem to involve "a question of sides," so that "it sounded very much like puss-in-the-corner, and she could only wonder if the distribution of parties would lead to a rushing to and fro and a changing of places." Life among the big folk seems one extended game of coupling off; taking her own initiative, Maisie joins the circle of players by tastefully pairing Sir Claude, her mother's "partner," and Mrs. Beale, her father's ex-governess second wife. Ironically, the most pleasing of all the available amorous combinations gets staged in part by the impact of Maisie's consistent game logic on the singularly immature adults who surround her.

This naïve play with the various permutations of the given figures is itself foresworn with the introduction of a brusque and self-consciously benign influence. Maisie is brought back from a peculiarly giddy moral holiday as she becomes increasingly aware of a new slant—the view from the "straighteners" perched atop the sensitive nose of Mrs. Wix, Maisie's devoted (and decidedly un-faery) godmother. Certain combinations of partners, it seems, are "bad." Yet when Maisie privately contemplates Mrs. Wix's approved arrangements, she notes with a telling childish irony that the "proper" pairs are "not of the age they ought to be."[14] What, in short, Maisie comes to recognize is that Mrs. Wix's moral sense discriminates in favor of "unnatural" alliances; it frustrates the interplay of inherently congenial beings. Where Mrs. Wix will only tolerate a cumbersome threesome (herself, Maisie, and Sir Claude), the perceptive young girl would plead for a more generous foursome, adding Mrs. Beale, to ensure the fullest concert of viable affections. In the idyllic calm of her French exile with Mrs. Wix, revelation comes:

> in a summer hum of French insects and a phase of almost somnolent reverie ... Maisie most had the vision of what it was to shut out from such a perspective so appealing a participant. [Mrs. Beale] It had not yet appeared so vast as at that moment, this prospect ... of courtesy in romantic forms.

To be sure, this idyllic vision is soon revoked by Maisie's final choice to remain alone with Mrs. Wix. But that choice is calculated to dissolve the untenable romantic foursome into a more perfect union of two separate and sufficient couples. In the end, the initiated Maisie emancipates cherished lives both from the artificial shackles of game logic and from the abrasive fetters of the "moral sense."

Much like Turgenev's Volodya, Maisie lays to rest her aggrieved childhood without calling to arms a moralistic retaliation against the betrayals perpetrated by adult sensuality. She, too, participates in a "clement vision" which acknowledges life's turbulent pool of energies without condemning its incessant inconstancy. What Maisie knows is that vital force will have its sway, that visceral stimuli and spontaneous responses impart an ongoing grace of interplay that "straighteners" can never petrify. "Maisie knew what 'amour' meant ... and wondered if Mrs. Wix did." Maisie Farange is graced with perception enough to celebrate her initiation to adult awareness: undismayed by life's incorrigible muddle, with her moral capacities intact, she rises to a state of aesthetic rapture resilient enough to withstand the random blows of fortune and the contrary listings of the human heart. Through Maisie, Henry James links hands with Ivan Turgenev in the practice of a visionary poetry of reconciliation to life's gross vitality. Volodya and Maisie epitomize a cherished heroism of perception; held captive to a universe of "realistic" assumptions, they nonetheless ascend to a plateau of consciousness which consecrates them as postapprenticeship "seers."[15] The narrative recording of their careers in perception is also an enactment of each author's vision of the aesthetic imagination as it makes its brave journey from bewilderment to bewonderment. In their shared disposition toward a clement vision of life's amoral flux of relations, Maisie and Volodya bear witness to the deep temperamental affinity, that "one much-embracing echo," which James himself heard resounding from Turgenev's modest structures into his own mammoth house of fiction.

The Clement Vision

Yet, that "echo" takes on a distinctively American quality as it reverberates in the compositions of Henry James. Good listening requires us to take pause and make some final discriminations. While it is true that Turgenev and James both celebrate envisaged states of consciousness which redeem and aestheticize "experience," their characteristic visions are attained from quite different standpoints. We can begin to locate the Jamesian vantage on a "clement vision" by citing his touching letter of consolation written to Grace Norton in 1883.[16]

> I don't know *why* we live ... consciousness is an illimitable power, and though at times it may seem to be all consciousness of misery, yet in the way it propagates itself from wave to wave, so that we never cease to feel ... there is something that holds one in one's place, makes it a standpoint in the universe which it is probably good not to forsake.... Don't melt too much into the universe, but be as solid and dense and fixed as you can.

James clearly imagines the reconciling vision as emanating from a *conscious individual act of discretion*, as well as from a natural perceptive gift. This means that the Jamesian visionary equanimity is purchased at a known and accepted cost; the price is a renunciation of possessing, or being possessed by, sensual experience. It is necessary to forswear the physical plunge into multiple experiences if one is to be free to perceive and contemplate the high arc of Experience Itself. Behind each Jamesian "clement vision," there is the willed "negative gesture" of a hero of perception: "it is as if experience were not discarded but negated and burned in the mind along with innocence, in a transcending *effort*."[17] The transformation of experiential bewilderment into aesthetic bewonderment requires a willingness to entertain life's entire prospect at an Olympian appreciative remove; one must summon the redemptive restraint which liberates the consciousness to savor its own activism as it experiences experience. Tony Tanner has nicely described the position and the posture of a representative Jamesian heroine of perception. "Just because she opened her eyes to all of it, just because of her honest wonder and interest, just because of her unprejudiced lucidity of vision, she seems to forfeit all rights of participation, all the privileges of consummation."[18] To some readers, the price of Jamesian bewonderment may seem too austere, or it may seem an arbitrary exaction levied against one's visceral humanity; but to the hero of perception, it is a voluntary truce that is embraced after long and dexterous negotiations with realism's limitations on human gratification. The Jamesian visionary posture represents the most intelligent bargain that can be struck by an apprentice to the school of experience.

The situation and posture of Turgenev's aesthetes and visionaries is, in comparison, not so enviable. Indeed, it might occur to some readers that the price Turgenev exacts for the capacity to poeticize experience is physical debilitation rather than an act of conscious renunciation. In Turgenev as in James, there is a necessary prehistory of deprivation or restraint behind the emergence of the clement vision; but Turgenev's visionaries have not so consciously bargained for their condition of redemptive remove. Typically, they are *unwittingly* disbarred from full sensual experience. Whether they be paralytics, simpletons, or bachelors, they yearn for a deep immersion in the alluring bath of pulsating phenomena they intuit exists.[19] When, to their astonishment, they succeed in experiencing an inundation in a "pansensory" awareness, they have attained the Turgenevan clement vision of experience. But unlike the Jamesian heroes of perception, they have not shaped themselves to their calling. Turgenev's aesthetic integration with life at large proceeds through the virtually miraculous restoration of a naïve, organic intuition of the biosphere's inhuman integrity and equilibrium. The Turgenevan visionary, however fractured or passive a personality, is the recipient of a total insight into the beautiful symmetry of life's deployment of vital energy. Though less heroically attained, this, too, is a vision which makes possible the perception of ultimate reality as a deeply poetic and pacifying interplay of forces in motion.

The visionary aesthetic of Henry James remains loyal to a voluntaristic psychology that is very American. The Jamesian visionary is ecstatic, but he or she is also brought toward salvation through mature obedience to a doctrine of good works. A life-style that accommodates a beatific comprehension of experience itself is consciously chosen. The Jamesian visionary, in a gesture of active good will, extends a benediction on the protean writhings of life; he is a benevolent speculator who is willing to invest his whole imagination in order to endow experience with appreciable form. Without great anxiety or melodramatic anguish, the arbitrariness of an imposed aesthetic shaping of experience is recognized.[20] Indeed, it is celebrated as a redemptive exercise of the "free spirit's" sovereign imagination.

By contrast, the visionary aesthetic of Ivan Turgenev springs from a fatalistic psychology. The leap into beatific perception is a sudden movement executed under the pressure of Grace. It follows the collapse of egocentric imagination and the involuntary abdication of "personalist" claims on experience. The Turgenevan visionary is first reduced to an utterly receptive will-less state before he or she miraculously expands with the afflatus for a vitalistic identification with the powers that hold sway. The wondrous holism of the organic universe is finally perceptible only to those eyes which are no longer animated by the spark of private appetite.

The conscientious "realist" in Turgenev and James never fails to measure the degree to which heroic aspirations invariably get stunted in the pelting they receive from unforeseen contingencies. But beyond the near horizon of disenchantment, there often opens out the imaginative prospect of a visionary second sight. By temperament, Turgenev and James are inclined to redeem adult experience, though they concede it is fundamentally disenchanting; as practicing poets of perception itself, they regularly affirm the capacity of the aesthetic faculty to place a clement construction (or an exquisite envelope of poetry) on the commonest truths of experience. The affinities between Turgenev and James are many, but they are particularly akin in this propensity for envisaging climactic victories of perception over inextricable predicament. Miracles of imaginative transubstantiation occur with impressive frequency in the recorded works of these two idiosyncratic poetic realists. A fully secular religion of consciousness begins to emerge in the passage of perception from Turgenev to James.

As Ernest Renan noted in his moving eulogy to Ivan Turgenev, it is the special mission of the "visionary realist" to be "like God in the Book of Job, who 'makes peace on the heights.' "[21] It may be that today this particular mission of pacification exudes a musty, valetudinarian odor. It may be that a strictly aesthetic redemption of experience is now well behind us. Recent times have clamored, often stridently, and with justice, for "commitment." But the so-called "genteel era" no less urgently demanded a composed sense of perspective. Within the decorous, well-ordered mansions of Turgenevan and Jamesian fiction, there was ample room to conduct an intensive campaign. Fundamentally, it was a humane struggle to liberate the aesthetic consciousness from the oppressive guardianship of the ethical conscience. By contrast, our historical priority would seem to be the need to reattach a normative conscience to a dangerously free-floating cult of consciousness. But unless we can empathize with the aesthetic emancipation undertaken by the great novelists' novelists, we shall impoverish our own openness to what Renan called "the era of the great amnesty" envisaged in Ivan Turgenev's posture toward disillusionment. And certainly literary historians without such an empathy will blind themselves to the controversial impact and the creative impulse which Turgenev once stimulated in the Anglo-American imagination. Fortunately, Henry James was a true connoisseur of the Russian master. By paying heed to his shrewd responses, we can perhaps restore our sight of Ivan Turgenev's clement vision of disenchanted, prosaic life. Perhaps, too, we can slowly cultivate a renewed appreciation for a redemptive art that knows "what to make of a diminished thing."

Notes

CHAPTER ONE

1. Davie, "Turgenev in England," p. 183.
2. Arthur Mizener, *The Sense of Life in the Modern Novel* (Boston, 1964), p. 5.
3. Harry Levin, *The Gates of Horn: A Study of Five French Realists* (New York, 1963), p. 34.
4. Donald Fanger, *Dostoevsky and Romantic Realism: A Study of Dostoevsky in Relation to Balzac, Dickens, and Gogol* (Chicago, 1967), p. 7.
5. Saul Bellow, "The Art of Fiction: An Interview," *The Paris Review* 36, p. 61.
6. Maurice Z. Schroder, "The Novel as a Genre," *Massachusetts Review* (Winter, 1963), pp. 292-94. See also Levin, pp. 48-52.
7. Auerbach, *Mimesis*, p. 416.
8. Fanger, *Dostoevsky and Romantic Realism*, pp. 14-15.
9. Sir Kenneth Clark, "Provincialism," Presidential Address, *The English Association* (London, 1962), pp. 4, 5.
10. Renato Poggioli, "The Tradition of Russian Realism," in *The Phoenix and The Spider* (Cambridge, Mass., 1957), pp. 1-14.
11. D. H. Lawrence, (Preface to Mastro-don Gesualdo by Giovanni Verga), in *Phoenix: The Posthumous Papers of D. H. Lawrence*, ed. Edward D. McDonald (New York, 1967), p. 227.

CHAPTER TWO

1. Hawthorne, "Agnosticism," p. 7. Hawthorne's recognition of the superior stylistic "texture" achieved by Turgenev, James, and Howells is all the more remarkable considering his religious discomfort over fictions devoid of ideality and "providential interferences."
2. Falk, "Literary Criticism," p. 123.
3. Howells, "Henry James, Jr.," pp. 25-29. The crucial passage, in part, reads: "The new school derives from Hawthorne and George Eliot ... but it studies human nature much more in its wonted aspects, and finds its ethical and dramatic examples in the operation of lighter but not really less vital motives. The moving accident is certainly not its trade. . . . It is largely influenced by French fiction in form; but it is the realism of Daudet rather than the realism of Zola." (p. 28)
4. The definitive study of Anglo-American cultural responses to the Russian novelist is Gettmann's *Turgenev in England and America*. Gettmann demonstrates that the initial British enthusiasm for Turgenev was a by-product of the Crimean War; Englishmen gratefully scanned Turgenev for socio-political data on the barbaric Slav. Aesthetically, the prevalent British attitude was to deride Turgenev for deficient plots, lack of incident, and unsatisfactory endings. Generally, his subject matter and pessimism were felt to be not quite wholesome. French and German responses will be touched upon in my discussion of the transmission of Turgenev to America.
5. Falk, *Victorian Mode*, p. 4.
6. Mott, *History of American Magazines*, p. 305.
7. Martin, *Harvests of Change*, p. 53. My discussion of the cultural ambiance of Reconstruction America is much indebted to this study, both for the informing particulars and the synoptic view it offers.
8. Falk, *Victorian Mode*, p. 26.
9. Haight, "Realism Defined," p. 880.
10. Poetic realism apparently arose, in theory and in practice, in Germany in

The Clement Vision

the 1830s. Otto Ludwig claimed that "it aims at artistic reproduction of reality, avoiding any illusion of vulgar factuality" and that it "stands midway between the objective truth of things and the law which our mind is impelled to read into them." It was a slogan embraced by writers intent upon conveying the "natural" feel of agrarian life, which combined a closeness to naturalistic detail with a spontaneous sense that "the only realities are the persuasions of the human mind." (See Silz, *Realism and Reality*, pp. 12-16.)

11.   Matthew Josephson, *Portrait of the Artist as American* (New York, 1930), p. 79.

12.   Mario Praz, "The Victorian Mood: A Reappraisal," in *Backgrounds to Victorian Literature*, ed. Richard A. Levine (San Francisco, 1967), p. 69.

13.   Cf. Roberts, *Henry James's Criticism*. Roberts describes the neophyte James as "an uncompromising foe of novelty and expansiveness in literature" (p. 8), and points out again and again, the similarity of James's reaction to the Flaubert *cénacle* with the attitudes of George Eliot's French partisans, Edmond Scherer and Ferdinand Brunetière.

14.   James, *Notes of a Son and Brother*, p. 56 (hereafter cited as *NSB*).

15.   Perry, who was two years the junior of Henry James, evoked a universal awe among the most cosmopolitan and learned of his contemporaries. James himself considered him an "exemplary" and "discouraging" friend: "he had let himself loose in the world of books, pressed and roamed through the most various literatures and the most voluminous authors, with a stride that, as it carried him beyond all view, left me dismayed and helpless at the edge of the forest." (*NSB*, p. 135) And Howells, in his "Recollections of an *Atlantic* Editorship" (1907), gratefully acknowledged "the very efficient and singularly instructed help of Mr. Thomas Sergeant Perry, who knew not only more of current continental literature than any other American, but more than all the other Americans."

16.   Mahieu, *Sainte-Beuve*, p. 101.

17.   Iknayan, *Idea of the Novel*, p. 23.

18.   DuVal, *Subject of Realism*, p. 117. Marguerite Iknayan paraphrases the *Revue*'s consistent position thus: "A novel should have a thought behind it, but not a specific philosophy.... And the thought must be general rather than particular, not scientific nor too detailed, so that the novelist remained more an artist than a thinker." (*Idea of the Novel*, p. 103.)

19.   Weinberg, *French Realism*, especially pp. 102, 118.

20.   DuVal, *The Subject of Realism*, pp. 130-37.

21.   Weinberg, *French Realism*, pp. 27-29.

22.   James, *NSB*, pp. 91, 87. John LaFarge (1835-1910) was the descendant of a family with Napoleonic loyalties which had fled to the United States as refugees from San Domingo's planter-military caste. Although raised in "Old New York," around Washington Square, LaFarge was fond of boasting that "the very furniture and hangings of the Empire parlor did not belong to the Victorian epoch in which I was growing up." His electric impact on the James brothers is recorded in the memoirs of their Newport neighbor, the future actor-playwright, James M. S. Mackaye. William announced to his brother and Perry: "There's a new fellow come to Hunt's class. He knows everything. He has read everything. He has seen everything—paints everything. He's a marvel." q.v. LeClair, *Young Henry James*, p. 285.

23.   For a brief, deft sketch of this history, see Demetz, "Defenses of Dutch Painting," pp. 97-115.

24.   Cortissoz, *John LaFarge*, p. 115. Henry James was lastingly impressed by these early exercises in perspectivism. LaFarge painted, he wrote, "with the implication, a hundred times beneficent and fertilizing, that if one didn't in these connections consistently take one's stand on super-subtlety of taste one was a helpless outsider ... a doctrine more salutary at that time in our world at large than any other that might be sounded." (*NSB*, pp. 97-98).

25.   Harlow, *Thomas Sergeant Perry*, p. 18.

26.   James, *NSB*, p. 316.

27.   Wellek, "Henry James's Literary Theory," p. 298.

28.   James, "French Critic," in *Notes and Reviews*, p. 104.

29. Irving Babbitt, *The Masters of Modern French Criticism* (Cambridge, Mass., 1912), p. 194. Babbitt called Scherer "probably the most accomplished cosmopolitan of his time" (p. 190), but goes on to point out that he was not averse to making appeals to common sense and tradition when his critical standards seemed in danger of being set adrift in his philosophy of flux.

30. Tremblay, *La Critique Littéraire*, p. 22. I am heavily indebted to this monograph for the particulars of Scherer's life and intellectual evolution.

31. James, *Notes and Reviews*, p. 106. Or, as Morris Roberts summed it all up: "The point is that Scherer was moralist, liberal, and man of the world. . . . It proved that one could be European, could be in the widest sense a man of taste and experience and still remain intellectually and morally respectable." (*Henry James's Criticism*, p. 13.)

32. Mahieu, *Sainte-Beuve*, p. 45n. Both, for instance, wrote cordially of Balzac and Eliot, while deploring Baudelaire and Zola.

33. Harlow, "Letters to Perry" in the appendix to her biography, pp. 282, 287.

34. Henry James, ed., *The Letters of William James*, Volume 1 (Boston, 1920), p. 106. William's literary awakening is perhaps best expressed in a letter of 1867 from Divonne: "I am struck more than ever I was with the hopelessness of us English, and *a fortiori* the Germans, ever competing with the French in matters of form or finite taste of any sort. They are sensitive to things that simply don't exist for us." (*NSB*, p. 449.)

35. "Gustave Droz," *Nation* 12 (1871), p. 130.

36. Cf. T. S. Perry's articles devoted to Cherbuliez in *Nation* 13 (1872), and in *Atlantic* 37 (1876).

37. Price, *Attitude of Freytag and Schmidt*, p. 108. My summary of Schmidt's critical stance is derived from this study.

38. Mérimée, who enjoyed a mutually profitable working relationship with Turgenev in which each would translate and correct for the other, contributed an influential article on the Russian in *Le Moniteur* of May 1868. In it, he recognized the poetic economy of Turgenev's painterly descriptions and the highly individuated precision of his character portraits, which were unflawed by moral commentary. He did, however, object to the accumulation of detail and the consequent retardation of plot in the novels. The article contains a memorable summation: "Il y a peu d'événements dans ses romans. Rien de plus simple que leur fable, rien qui ressemble plus à la vie ordinaire." See *Portraits Historiques*, p. 343.

39. Price, *Attitude of Freytag and Schmidt*, p. 20.

40. See Perry's review of Volume 4 of Schmidt's *Bilder* in *Atlantic* 35 (1875), p. 505.

41. Harlow, *Thomas Sergeant Perry*, p. 46. There seems to be some confusion as to when Howells and Perry actually met. Miss Harlow has Henry James introducing them in the autumn of 1869, whereas Edwin H. Cady in *Road to Realism* has them crossing paths no later than the summer of 1869 in Quebec. (p. 182) In any case, Howells, via James, was surely well informed about Perry's "deep researches" into novels.

42. Howells, ed., *Life in Letters*, p. 379.

43. "While for Henry James, the revelation of this artistic method came from Ivan Turgenev, Howells already had been weighing the advantages of the dramatic method three years before the great Russian was available to him." Carter, *Howells and Realism*, p. 123.

44. Haertel, "German Literature," pp. 46-49.

45. See Howells's review of *Edelweiss* in *Atlantic* 23 (1869), p. 762.

46. Fryckstedt, *In Quest of America*, p. 82. The essay itself has been reprinted in Rudolph and Clara Marburg Kirk's edition of *Criticism and Fiction and Other Essays* (New York, 1959), p. 104-09.

47. Matthiessen, *James Family*, p. 548.

48. Perry's evaluation was made in his review of a German translation of Pisemsky's *Thousand Souls* in *Atlantic* 27 (1871), p. 266. Schmidt's equivalent verdict can be found on the last page of his essay on Turgenev in the *Bilder*, I, pp. 429-70.

49.   This essay, which appeared in Volume 4 of the *Bilder* (1875), is excerpted in: *Inostrannaya Kritika o Turgeneve* (St. Petersburg, 1884), a necrology collection published by Y. I. Ragozin. See especially pp. 14-15.

50.   Review of *On the Eve* in *Nation* 12 (1871), pp. 340-41.

51.   Besides publishing reviews of 350 novels from 1871-81 in *Atlantic* and *Nation*, Perry translated some of Turgenev's finest short stories for *Galaxy* and *Lippincott's*, and served as *de facto* editor of *North American Review* for 1873-74, soliciting Henry James's first essay on Turgenev. See Harlow, *Thomas Sergeant Perry*, pp. 37, 40, 65.

52.   For biographical details on this fascinating minor figure, see Glasrud, *Hjalmar Hjorth Boyesen*

53.   Boyesen, "A Visit," pp. 456-66.

54.   G. P. Lathrop, "Growth of the Novel," pp. 684-97.

55.   Lathrop, "Novel" pp. 313-24.

56.   McMahon, *Criticism of Fiction*, p. 30.

57.   Cited in Kirk and Kirk, *Criticism and Fiction*, p. 112.

58.   For a brief survey of the impact of relativism on fiction, see Lionel Stevenson, "The Relativity of Truth in Victorian Fiction," in *Victorian Essays: A Symposium*, ed. Warren D. Anderson and Thomas D. Clareson (Oberlin, Ohio, 1967), pp. 71-86. On the evolution of "dramatic method" Stevenson observes: "The maturing of the relationship between writer and reader chanced to coincide with the growing realization that truth was relative and that the old established verities had dissolved. into bewildering flux." (pp. 75-76).

CHAPTER THREE

1.   See Howells's review of *French Poets and Novelists* (hereinafter cited as *FPN*) in *Atlantic Monthly* (July 1878), reproduced in *Discovery of a Genius: William Dean Howells and Henry James*, ed. Albert Mordell (New York, 1961), p. 82.

2.   The original text is "Ivan Turgéniew" in *North American Review* 118 (1874), pp. 326-56.

3.   Consider the virtually confessional notes struck at the end of James's "Turgéniew":

> If he were a dogmatic optimist we suspect that, as things go, we should long ago have ceased to miss him from our library. . . . To our usual working mood the world is apt to seem Mr. Turgéniew's hard world, and when, at moments, the strain and the pressure deepen, the ironical element figures not a little in our form of address to those short-sighted friends who have whispered that it is an easy one.

This shared form of address toward life was duly noted in an early review by George Saintsbury:

> The paper might, perhaps, be better entitled "The Characteristics of a Novelist, as exhibited in Ivan Turgénieff," and it contains some interesting hints as to Mr. James's views of his own function. (*The Academy*: April 20, 1878, p. 338.)

4.   Mordell, *Discovery*, p. 83.

5.   Pacey, "Henry James," p. 241.

6.   James obviously prefers to judge de Musset "with all kinds of allowances and indulgences" and in memorializing Gautier he is similarly disposed "to large allowances." See James, *FPN*, pp. 2, 33. (Hereafter all pagination references from this text will be included parenthetically in the chapter itself).

7.   Perhaps the strongest indictment of the "strangely loveless" British "comprehensive fictions" occurs in the essay on Mme. Sand: "few persons would

resort to English prose fiction for any information concerning the ardent forces of the heart—for any ideas upon them." (p. 172).

8.   For a full discussion of the implications of this term, the reader can consult the chapter on "Felt Life" in Lebowitz, *Imagination of Loving*, pp. 21-53.

9.   James, *Partial Portraits*, p. 322.

10.   James, *FPN*, pp. 216, 222.

11.   One might cite as evidence such rapturous statements as: "if there are no heroines we see more distinctly, there are none we love more ardently. It would be difficult to point, in the blooming fields of fiction, to a group of young girls more radiant with maidenly charm." (216) Or again, "these fair Muscovites have a spontaneity, an independence, quite akin to the English ideal of maiden loveliness." (220)

12.   Compare James's similar frustration when faced with the real-life lack of moral imagination among Englishwomen in Great Malvern society *ca.* 1870: "I revolt from their dreary deathly want of—what shall I call it?—Clover Hooper has it—intellectual grace—Minny Temple has it—moral spontaneity. They live wholly in the realm of the cut and dried." q.v. Lubbock, *Letters*, p. 26.

13.   Matthiessen, *James Family*, p. 549.

14.   James, "Daniel Deronda," in *Partial Portraits*, p. 77 (hereafter cited as *PP*).

15.   James, "The Novels of George Eliot," (1866) in Le Roy Phillips, ed., *Views and Reviews* (Boston, 1908), pp. 5-6.

16.   Ibid., p. 37.

17.   James, "Middlemarch," (1873) in Leon Edel, ed., *The Future of the Novel* (New York, 1956), p. 89.

18.   Cf. T. S. Perry on *Middlemarch* in *North American Review* 116: (April 1873), pp. 432-40, where Eliot is summarized as "an author who, apparently, prefers a long and even monotonous narration . . . to an artificially rounded story where dramatic effect is sought." (438)

19.   See especially Scherer's own extended conversation about *"Daniel Deronda"* included in *Etudes* 5. The specific caveat that concludes this review essay is often rephrased in James's comments on Eliot in *PP.*: "point de grand art sans philosophie, et cependant point de plus dangereux ennemi de l'art que la réflexion." (p. 304).

20.   *PP*, pp. 78, 84.

21.   Ibid., p. 89.

22.   Henry James, *Letters of William James* I, pp. 182, 185.

23.   Kelley, *Early Development*, p. 196, boldly claims that Turgenev was the "main reason" why James came to Paris in late 1875. One ought not to forget that James had wangled a commission to write a series of Paris letters for the *New York Tribune*, providing reason enough to haunt the city. Yet there is cause to suspect an anterior reason behind James's acceptance of so burdensome a commission. We know, from letters to his father, that Henry was bitterly disappointed at having missed Turgenev at Baden-Baden in the summer of 1874. And we also know that he was searching for virtually any means to get to Paris in 1875. (See Leon Edel, *Conquest of London*, pp. 171-72, 193-95).

24.   Lubbock, *Letters of Henry James*, p. 39.

25.   Ibid., p. 51. Once he crossed the Channel, James's perspective characteristically changed. He saw the positive side of the contrast and somewhat boastfully announced to Grace Norton: "To tell the truth, I find myself a good deal more of a cosmopolitan than the average Briton of culture." (p. 55).

26.   Edel, *Conquest of London*, p. 220.

27.   Howells, *Life in Letters*, p. 215.

28.   Harlow, *Thomas Sergeant Perry*, p. 291.

29.   Ibid., p. 293.

30.   Edel, *Conquest of London*, p. 269.

31.   Guy de Maupassant, in his obituary notice on Turgenev, has left us what is perhaps the best account of the Russian's position in the eyes of his young confrères:

In spite of his age and of the fact that his career was almost at an end, he had the most modern and advanced literary ideas, rejecting all forms of the old, obviously mechanical novel ... and only asking for life, nothing but life—'slices of life'—without complications or wonderful adventures. "The novel," he used to say, "is now gradually freeing itself from the stage tricks upon which it relied at first ... it is for us to reject all such inferior and artificial methods, while at the same time simplifying and elevating an art which is in its essence the art of life." (Cited in Halperine-Kaminsky, *Tourgéneff and His French Circle*, pp. 242-43.)

32. Edel, *Conquest of London*, p. 236.
33. Lubbock, *Letters of Henry James*, p. 49.
34. Later reprinted as "Ivan Turgénieff" in *PP*, pp. 291-322. It is also available in *The Art of Fiction*, ed. Morris Roberts (New York, 1948), pp. 97-116. (All my pagination references are from the 1888 text).
35. Edel, *Middle Years*, p. 76 (Italics added).
36. Henry James, "Alphonse Daudet," in *Century* 26: (August, 1883), pp. 498-509. (All further pagination citations are from this text).
37. Frierson and Edwards, "Impact of French Naturalism," p. 1012.
38. Edel, *Middle Years*, p. 95. The intermediary was Theodore (T. E.) Child, who somewhat startled the *Atlantic* readership in May by reporting that James had claimed "the average Frenchman is infinitely sharper in his observations than the average Englishman or American: he takes in more details; he is more appreciative of *nuances* and shades." (p. 99)
39. James, "Ivan Turgenef's New Novel," p. 252.
40. Lubbock, *Letters of Henry James*, p. 109.
41. Roberts, *Henry James's Criticism*, p. 31.
42. Ibid., p. 35
43. "The Art of Fiction," in Edel, *Future of the Novel*, pp. 20, 27.
44. From a letter to Vernon Lee (Viola Paget) acknowledging the receipt of her *Miss Brown*, as cited in Edel, *Middle Years*, p. 117. (Italics added).
45. Cited as "Turgenev and Tolstoy" (actually part of an 1897 James preface to a translated edition of Turgenev) in Edel, *Future of the Novel*, pp. 229-30.

CHAPTER FOUR

1. Edel, *Conquest of London*, pp. 128-29.
2. This preliminary sketch of the basic fable behind the "international theme" is based upon S. Gorley Putt's distinction between James's "passionate pilgrim" types and Christopher Newman of *The American* who "is never really sensitive to the lure of European cultural charm" and is not a *willing* victim of cosmopolitan infatuations. See his *Henry James: A Reader's Guide*, p. 110.
3. Edel, *Conquest of London*, pp. 171-72.
4. Ibid., pp. 174-75.
5. *The Selected Letters of Henry James*, ed. Leon Edel (New York, 1955), pp. 72-73.
6. q.v. Lerner, "Influence of Turgenev on James," pp. 28-54. This study, while containing much information, is an unfortunate example of indiscriminate, mechanical juxtaposition of titles, themes, and characters. For instance, Turgenev's "A Strange Story"—a sober study of one variety of religious experience—is coupled with the satiric "Professor Fargo" because both tales happen to deal with spiritualist mediums. Turgenev's two-way exchange, "A Correspondence," is coupled with James's polylogue, "A Bundle of Letters," because both belong to the epistolary genre and share similar titles. A much more likely "germ" for the James story would be Gustave Droz's "Un Paquet de Lettres," reviewed by T. S. Perry in *The Nation* 12 (1871), p. 129. Finally, it is naïve to suppose, as Lerner does, that James had to go to Turgenev to learn the effectiveness of an antithetical pairing of "light" and "dark" heroines!
7. Edna Kenton, "Introduction," in *Eight Uncollected Tales of Henry James*

(New Brunswick, N.J., 1950), p. 4. Of the eighteen tales James wrote from 1869 to 1877, sixteen were in some form of first-person narration.

8.   The term is from Friedman, "Point of View," p. 1174.

9.   Kelly, *Early Development*, p. 148.

10.   I am here invoking a distinction between "fable" and "plot" first elaborated in Russian formalist criticism by Viktor Shklovsky in particular. The "fable" (*fabula*) is here understood to denote the basic story stuff yet to be related in the accomplished fictional narrative; the term generously embraces all the anecdotal raw materials as they exist *prior to* their actual narrative construction as a "plot." For the definitive English explication of this helpful and subtle conceptual distinction, consult Victor Erlich, *Russian Formalism: History-Doctrine* (The Hague, 1965), pp. 240-42.

11.   James, *FPN*, p. 218. This story appeared as "Le Brigadier" in that much-mentioned volume in James family correspondence, *Nouvelles Moscovites*, first published by Hetzel in May, 1869. Turgenev himself translated this story for that edition. For proof, see the documentation of R. M. Gorokhova in *Turgenevskii Sbornik* I, ed. M. P. Alekseev, pp. 268-69.

12.   James, *Selected Letters*, p. 72.

13.   For the full discussion of "A Correspondence" as symptomatic of Turgenev's occasionally unpalatable pessimism, see *FPN*, pp. 245-52. T. S. Perry published a translation of this story in *Galaxy* for 1871.

14.   James, *FPN*, p. 230.

15.   Ibid., p. 236 gives the clue, and an extensive discussion follows on pp. 237-42. James most likely read the work first in the German translation, *Frühlingsfluten*, which appeared late in 1872 in the sixth volume of the Mittau edition of Turgenev's works. By summer 1873, Hetzel had published a French version in a separate volume, *Les Eaux Printanières.*

16.   An especially strident protest was registered by Hetzel, Turgenev's French publisher, who accused him of falling in the dismal shadow of Mérimée, or worse, the "new school":

> Mais dissoudre, mais délayer une perle dans du vinaigre de toilette, ne me parait pas très bien imaginé . . . Le sujet moral, tout le monde n'a pas la force de l'aborder . . . de peur de plat on se refuse quelquefois le chef-d'oeuvre.

See A. Parménie et C. Bonnier de la Chapelle, *Histoire d'Un Éditeur et de ses Auteurs: P-J. Hetzel* (Paris, 1953), pp. 566-67.

17.   From P. V. Annenkov's reaction in a letter of 26 December, 1871, cited in the Addenda to Volume 11 of the *Polnoe Sobranie Sochinenii* [Complete Collected Works] of Turgenev, p. 462.

18.   See Howells's review in *Atlantic Monthly* 34, p. 231.

19.   When making "ideal comparisons" rather than functional juxtapositions to determine textual influences, I shall signal so by referring to the Russian title in the text. In this particular case, all citations are translated from the Russian *Collected Works in Ten Volumes*, Vol. 8 (Moscow, 1962), pp. 29-141.

20.   The one study that sufficiently recognizes the extent and purpose of Turgenev's deliberate hypertrophy of artistic allusions in depicting the Frankfurt romance is Matlaw, "Turgenev's Art in Spring Torrents," pp. 157-71. I could not agree more that "Each of these characters assumes that attitudes portrayed in art are indices of his own behaviour, and in each case this clashes with reality. . . . Incisive judgments on art and reality are first made when Polozova appears." (p. 164) For further documentation of the tissue of artifices constituting the "charm" of the relationship, consult the extensive notes to the text in volume 11 of the 1966 Moscow edition, pp. 474-87.

21.   Kelley, *Early Development*, pp. 163-64.

22.   All pagination references are from the 1875 *A Passionate Pilgrim* text as reproduced in *The Complete Tales of Henry James*, 3, ed. Leon Edel (London, 1962), pp. 299-350. In the French version Polozova is garbed at first "en robe de soie blanche" with "épais cheveux chatains"—see J. Tourguéneff *Les Eaux Printanières*, p. 153.

23. Spender, "School of Experience," p. 421.
24. The emphasis is mine. Note how this early fictional voice accurately forecasts the confident authorial assertion in "The Art of Fiction" that imagination and empathy *are* experiential components:

> The power to guess the seen from the unseen, to trace the implication of things, to judge the whole piece by the pattern, the condition of feeling life in general so completely that you are on your way to understanding any particular corner of it—this cluster of gifts may almost be said to constitute experience.... If experience consists of impressions, it may be said that impressions *are* experience. (p. 13)

25. See Krieger, *Tragic Vision*, p. 256.
26. Christof Wegelin has argued that James's location of "the trouble with Europe" *within* archetypal ingenuous Americans occurs first in "Madame de Mauves," but that conventional images of Europe do not themselves become the regular subject matter until the 1876 *Portraits of Places* series. See his *Image of Europe*, pp. 45, 28-29.
27. The only other instance of a self-incriminating fictional autobiographer is the narrator of "A Light Man" (1869). Yet the disengaged witness narrators in the other early tales are clearly spokesmen of limited reliability, too. James's onlookers are constantly filtering rather prosaic plot events through a self-mystifying imagination. For an admittedly clear example, see "At Isella" (1871) where the Italian cast gladly whets the romance-making, intrigue-shaping notions of the *Inglese* narrator. In "Eugene Pickering" the worldly narrator dramatically, but falsely, blackens the reputation of Mme. Blumenthal. I find myself sharply aware of the refracting medium of each narrator's voice, and never wholly trust the capsule verdicts offered by the onlookers, worldly or unworldly. Therefore, I fail to comprehend, let alone endorse, the certainty with which Krishna Balda Vaid asserts that "to avoid ambiguity James almost always has the intuitive flights of his narrators corroborated by subsequent events." For Vaid's view of the early Jamesian narrator as a neutral device rather than as a characterized presence, see his *Technique in Tales of Henry James*, pp. 14-18.
28. All citations refer to the pagination in *The Complete Tales*, 4 (London 1962), pp. 389-426. This text is based on the book publication of the tale in *The Madonna of the Future* (1879).
29. Leavis, "The Stories," p. 226.
30. James, *Selected Letters*, p. 73. In French *Le Journal d'un Homme de Trop* was translated by the author with Louis Viardot. It first appeared in the *RDM* (Dec. 1, 1861), then was included in the Hetzel edition of *Dimitri Roudine* (1862).
31. As signaled by the Russian title, all further references and page citations are taken from the canonical text as reprinted in the 1961 *Collected Works*, 5, pp. 139-79. Care will be taken to make no point that could have been lost in the Hetzel translation.
32. For a very sophisticated discussion of the rhetorical mix in Chulkaturin's self-defining verbal style, see Gabel', "Dnevnik Lishnego Cheloveka," pp. 121-23.
33. The entire duel script, including Chulkaturin's self-image as "morally murdered" by the opponent's gallant clemency, is a parodistic reenactment of Pushkin's tale, "The Shot."
34. Ezra Pound, "A Retrospect," in *Literary Essays of Ezra Pound* (London, 1960), p. 4.
35. All pagination references are taken from the Russian text reprinted in *Collected Works*, 5, (Moscow, 1961), pp. 180-203. The James text is that of the 1879 English edition of *Daisy Miller* (which included "Four Meetings") as republished in *The Complete Tales*, 4, (London, 1962), pp. 87-118.
36. M. Samarin, "Tema Strasti v Turgeneve," in *Tvorcheskii Put' Turgeneva*, ed. N. L. Brodskii, p. 130.
37. Here the question puzzling the reader is how to take the lack of

"denitiation" into experience. Is Miss Spencer's apparent serenity a triumph or a travesty of the way of renunciation? For a persuasive argument in favor of the latter, see Robert J. Griffin, "Notes Toward an Exegesis: 'Four Meetings,' " in *University of Kansas City Review* 29 (1962), pp. 45-49.

38.   A well-argued plea for recognizing Winterbourne as the structural center of James's most notorious "study" is Gargano, "Daisy Miller," pp. 114-20. In my discussion, all citations are based on the 1879 book edition text as reprinted in *Complete Tales*, 4, pp. 141-207.

39.   V. M. Fisher, "Povest' i Roman u Turgeneva," p. 16.

40.   All translations are mine and they follow the text and pagination in the Moscow *Collected Works*, 6, (1962), pp. 164-200.

41.   For a parallel line of argument, see John H. Randall III, "The Genteel Reader and *Daisy Miller*," in *American Quarterly* 17 (1965), p. 578: "The picturesque is the killer here; like any form of sentimentality, when overdone it can mislead people into being extremely cruel."

42.   James, *The Art of the Novel*, p. 270. Coincidentally, the appearance of Turgenev's Asya produced a controversial "flap" very similar to the hot reception granted James's typical American girl. Two of Turgenev's closest literary advisers, Botkin and Fet, felt that Asya was "made up" in the worst sense, an incredible composite of the normal feminine graces and an uncustomary license in self-expression. See the commentaries in Volume 7 of the 1964 Moscow *Complete Collected Works*, especially pp. 434-37, for details on Asya's private reception.

43.   I would agree with, and extend to *Asya*, the following verdict on the position of the authorial imagination: "the accumulation of his specific ironies hints at an ideal of freedom and of vitality and also of aesthetic and social awareness that is nowhere fully exemplified in the nouvelle." See Carol Ohmann, "Daisy Miller: A Study of Changing Intentions," in *American Literature* 36 (1964), p. 6.

44.   Viola Dunbar, "A Note on the Genesis of Daisy Miller," in *Philological Quarterly* 27 (1948), pp. 184-86. Also, Edward Stone, "Daisy Miller and Cherbuliez," in *PQ* 29 (1950), pp. 213-16.

45.   The elaborate obscurity covering the genesis and shape of the "international theme" can be portrayed vividly enough with a few examples. James and Howells outdid one another in according the other the honor of having invented the American prototype, Howells citing *The Passionate Pilgrim* in his 1882 *Century* article (p. 27) and James nominating Florida Vervain and Kitty Ellison as the first intensively American girls in his *Nation* review of *A Foregone Conclusion* (January 7, 1875). Later investigators have unearthed the precursor in James's "Travelling Companions" of 1870 (Fryckstedt, p. 147), in Turgenev (Kelley, p. 269), in Cooper and Hawthorne (Marius Bewley's *The Complex Fate*), in N. P. Willis (Wegelin in *PMLA* 77, pp. 805-10), and in the Parisian melodramas of Augier and Dumas, fils (Cargill). By far the best summary paper is Cargill, "First International Novel," pp. 418-25.

46.   Cargill discusses contemporary French "intrusion plots" on p. 422. For a sketch of the term "transplantation plot," see Dupee, *Henry James*, p. 128. For the morphology of traditional comic patterns of intrusion consult Frye, *Anatomy of Criticism*, pp. 43-49, 163-86.

47.   James, *Art of the Novel*, Preface to "The Reverberator," p. 187.

CHAPTER FIVE

1.   For instance, the latest edition of Bowker's *Books In Print* lists only two major scholarly titles on Turgenev: Yarmolinsky's critical biography and Richard Freeborn's important critical analysis, both of which, even in revised editions, date from 1960 to 1961.

2.   Turgenev's review is of *The Niece (Plemiannitsa)* by Evgeniia Tur'. The passage is cited in Brodskii, *I. S. Turgenev*, p. 111.

3.   An interesting discussion of the history of critics' confusions and

The Clement Vision

Turgenev's own vacillations regarding the distinction between *roman* and *povest'* in his works can be found in A. Batiuto, *Turgenev-Romanist* (Leningrad, 1972), pp. 240-52.

4.   I. S. Turgenev to I. A. Goncharov, April 7, 1859, in *Pisma*, III (Moscow-Leningrad, 1961), p. 290.

5.   Turgenev, *Sobranie Sochinenii*, X, p. 292.

6.   Freeborn, *Turgenev*, p. 64.

7.   Mudrick, "Character and Event in Fiction," pp. 214-15.

8.   Boyesen, "A Visit," p. 462.

9.   From Taine to Lukacs, the presence of a "type" has been the categorical criterion of literary "realism"; it is symptomatic of this particular tradition to regard the type as a synthetic figure which *concretizes* a conceptual realization in an individual personality. In Lukacs's view, "what makes it a type is that in it all the humanly and socially essential determinants are present on their highest level of development . . . rendering concrete the peaks and limits of men and epochs." (*Studies*, p. 6.) On Taine, see René Wellek, *A History of Modern Criticism*, IV (New Haven, 1965), p. 41. And for an excellent discussion of Balzac's "peculiar" and fortunately unsuccessful attempt to reduce his characters to "mere representativeness," see Bersani, *Balzac to Beckett*, pp. 33-35.

10.   Poirier, *Comic Sense*, p. 202.

11.   Lionel Trilling, "Princess Casamassima," pp. 58-60.

12.   Edward Engelberg, "James and Arnold: Conscience and Consciousness in a Victorian 'Kunstlerroman,' " *Criticism* 10 (1968), p. 94. An important confirmation of the notion that worldly experience is formative and socially integrating in the major European "novels of apprenticeship" may be found in Jost's authoritative "La Tradition Du Bildungsroman," pp. 97-115. In a central passage, Jost asserts, "l'important est de profiter des leçons du monde. Dans le roman d'aventures les événements éprouvent et vieillissent le héros, dans le roman d'apprentissage ils le marquent, le forment d'une façon définitive, cristallisent son caractère. La confrontation du héros avec son milieu, voilà le Bildungsprinzip goéthéen." (p. 99)

13.   Pritchett, *Living Novel*, pp. 387-88, 384. Incidentally, the second of Pritchett's points is broadly endorsed by Richard Freeborn. "Processes of growth and change in human terms seem to be forever inhibited by an essential changelessness of nature, and it is the conflict between these two forces, of inertia and motion, which becomes the dominant preoccupation of the Russian novel." See *Rise of the Russian Novel*, p. 123

14.   Freeborn, *Turgenev*, p. 156.

15.   Gippius, "O kompozitsii turgenevskikh romanov," p. 38.

16.   Freeborn, *Turgenev*, pp. 53-54.

17.   Cargill, "First International Novel," p. 419.

18.   Cargill, *Novels of Henry James*, p. 46.

19.   The description of the kernel of a "fate-tragedy" is from Bennett and Waidson, *History of the German Novelle*, p. 195.

20.   Tseitlin, *Masterstvo Turgeneva-Romanista*, pp. 211-12.

21.   For a fascinating discussion of Turgenev's fundamental attachment to an eighteenth-century aesthetic of control, delicacy, and symmetry, consult Grossman, *Portret Manon Lesko*. Grossman actually asserts that Turgenev "reveals his lengthy artistic achievement as being basically a re-working of the eighteenth-century domestic drama." (p. 12)

22.   Woodcock, "The Elusive Ideal," p. 45.

23.   L. V. Pumpianskii, "Turgenev i Zapad," in Brodskii, *I. S. Turgenev*, p. 93. Pumpianskii rightly points to George Sand as an important precursor of the Turgenevan novelistic form.

24.   This definition of the central strategy of a novella is from Silz, *Realism and Reality*, p. 6.

25.   Bourget, *Nouveaux Essais*, p. 209.

26.   Ward, *Search for Form*, especially pp. 31-35, 52.

CHAPTER SIX

1. James, *Art of the Novel*, p. 4. (Page references for further quotations from this Preface are given in parentheses)
2. *FPN*, pp. 224, 227, 228.
3. W. E. Henley on *Roderick Hudson* in *The Academy* (August 9, 1879), p. 99.
4. *FPN*, p. 223. This Rudin prototype for Roderick was established in Kelley, p. 188; other Turgenev precursors to the cast in *Roderick Hudson* are offered in Cargill, *Novels of Henry James*, pp. 22-23.
5. James, *Roderick Hudson*, p. 479. Future citations are extracted both from this edition and from the Harper Torchbook reprint of the 1909 revised edition (New York, 1960). Paginations will be documented in the text, with an "R" appended to indicate reference to the 1909 edition. The revised edition is cited only when its text elucidates vague phrasings in the initial narrative.
6. Leavis, "Henry James's First Novel," p. 297.
7. K. K. Istomin, "Roman *Rudin*: iz istorii turgenevskogo stilia" in Brodskii, *Tvorcheskii Put' Turgeneva*, p. 87.
8. Poirier, *Comic Sense*, p. 22.
9. Ibid., p. 11
10. For an intelligent discussion of James's conscious use of these Arnoldian antitheses, see Engelberg, "James and Arnold," p. 101.
11. Bialy, *Turgenev*, p. 68.
12. James, *Art of the Novel*, p. 15.
13. Cargill, *Novels of Henry James*, p. 29
14. James, *FPN*, pp. 227-28.
15. The hint is lightly dropped in Cargill, p. 23.
16. Engelberg, "James and Arnold," pp. 95, 110-11. The author's enthusiasm extends so far as to claim that *Roderick Hudson* is "the first serious *Kunstlerroman* in English"—an honor that just among the American claimants would have to be conceded to Melville for his *Pierre* (1852).
17. For a chronology of the genesis of Rudin's "rehabilitation," including the apparently pivotal event of reading Chernyshevsky's dissertation on "The Aesthetic Relations of Art and Reality," see G. V. Prokhorov's previously cited article in Brodskii, *I. S. Turgenev*, pp. 125-28.
18. Letter to I. F. Mnitskii (24 May 1853), in *Polnoe Sobranie Pisem*, II p. 150.
19. Henri Granjard, *Ivan Tourguénev*, p. 216
20. James, *Art of the Novel*, p. 43.
21. Ibid., p. 44.
22. Ibid., p. 47.
23. Ibid., p. 33 (from the preface to *The American*)
24. Boyesen, "A Visit," p. 462; refer to the citation quoted in Chapter V.
25. F. R. Leavis, " 'The Europeans': The Novel as Dramatic Poem" in *Scrutiny* 15 (1948), p. 209. The suggestion has been made that *The Europeans* reads like a prose version of Turgenev's "false idyll" for the stage, *A Month in the Country*—see Peter Buitenhuis, "Comic Pastoral: Henry James's The Europeans," in *University of Toronto Quarterly* 31 (1962), p. 153.
26. Kelley, *Early Development*, pp. 281-82.
27. The best known discussions of the derivation are in Kelley, *Early Development* (239-41); in Lerner, *Influence* (43-44); and in Phelps, *Russian Novel*, pp. 79-81.
28. James, *FPN*, pp. 230-31.
29. James, *Art of the Novel*, pp. 37.
30. From Turgenev's review of A. N. Ostrovsky's *Bednaia Nevesta* [The Poor Bride] in *Polnoe Sobranie Sochineniia*, V, p. 391.
31. Kurliandskaia, "Problema kharaktera v romanakh Turgeneva," p. 77.
32. Bialy, *Turgenev*, p. 91.
33. James, *FPN*, pp. 224-25, 225-26.

147

34. James, *PP*, p. 89.
35. James, *Art of the Novel*, p. 51.
36. Hardy, *Appropriate Form*, pp. 18, 21.
37. Poirier, *Comic Sense*, pp. 42-43.
38. Kelley, *Early Development*, p. 296.
39. Rourke, *American Humor*, pp. 202-03. The original edition was published in 1931.
40. James, *FPN*, p. 251.

CHAPTER SEVEN

1. Bourget, *Nouveaux Essais*, p. 233.
2. Turgenev's "philosophical" reputation for an acutely pessimistic and incapacitating fatalism has become legendary. An intelligent recent reassertion of Turgenev's absorption in an unredeemed fatalism is Eva Kagan-Kans, "Fate and Fantasy: A Study of Turgenev's Fantastic Stories," *Slavic Review* 28 (1969), 543-60. As for James, his alleged fixation on finally irremediable "deprivations" and his cult of conscious resignation—themes insisted upon by F. O. Matthiessen in 1944—have been given fresh currency in Sears's *Negative Imagination*.
3. I have borrowed the terminological distinction from Damian Grant's lucid contribution to Methuen and Company's "Critical Idiom" series—*Realism*. The differentiation is between narratives which consciously promote a reader's deference to empirical "evidence" or to perceptual "self-evidence": "Truth may accordingly be seen as either scientific or poetic; discovered by a process of knowing or created by a process of making." p. 9.
4. From a letter of August 7, 1874, in Jean Seznec, "Lettres de Tourguéneff à Henry James," *Comparative Literature* 1 (1949), p. 198.
5. From James's review of *Virgin Soil*, reproduced in *Literary Reviews and Essays*, ed. Albert Mordell, (New York, 1957), pp. 191, 192.
6. Defending Newman's defeat in *The American*, James explained to his editor, Howells: "I suspect it is the tragedies in life that arrest my attention . . . and say more to my imagination." (*Selected Letters*, pp. 68-69). On Hyacinth Robinson, see Hamilton, "James's *Princess Casamissima* and Turgenev's *Virgin Soil*," pp. 354-64.
7. James, *Future of the Novel*, pp. 229-30.
8. Ibid., p. 233.
9. An excellent summary statement on Jamesian perceptual realism may be found in Tanner, *Reign of Wonder*, especially on p. 268.

"James is not interested in communicating directly to the reader what actually happened in the way of material incident. Nor is he interested in showing us the possible discrepancies between what actually happened and the sensitive girl's impression of what happened. Rather, he wants to involve us in the moment-by-moment efforts on the part of the candid outsider to discern and decide, to infer and interpret. Not the facts, but the facts saturated with the deciphering efforts and emotional predispositions of a proximate, involved naivety."

10. In the discussion that follows, I have reference to the text of *Pervaya Lyubov'* included in Volume 6 of Ivan Turgenev, *Sobranie Sochinenii v desiati tomakh*. All translations are my own. The text of *What Maisie Knew* is from the New York edition of 1909, as reprinted in the Anchor edition of 1954.
11. See Brodianski, "Turgenev's Short Stories," p. 84.
12. James, *Art of the Novel*, p. 143.
13. James, "Turgéniew," p. 335.
14. J. A. Ward has an especially interesting discussion of "Maisie's morality of aesthetic propriety": "She has the child's unquestioning acceptance of the arbitrary yet systematic rules of play . . . most of Maisie's judgments are rooted in

an idea of form. These formal judgments represent a kind of improvised morality." Maisie has, in short, a healthy sense of proportion and beauty if not quite Mrs. Wix's "moral sense." *Search for Form*, pp. 157-62.

15.   On Maisie as an archetypal Jamesian "knower," see Snow, "Pattern of Innocence," pp. 235-36. For proof of the autobiographical elements that inform Volodya's depiction, consult André Mazon, *Manuscrits Parisiens d'Ivan Tourguénev* (Paris, 1930), pp. 20-21.

16.   *Letters of Henry James*, I, pp. 100-01.

17.   Cambon, "Negative Gesture," p. 340.

18.   Tanner, *Reign of Wonder*, p. 302.

19.   Repeatedly, Turgenev's melancholic hunter-narrator in the numerous "sportsman's sketches" encounters an awesome, yet also pacifying, spectacle: a form of life reduced to a minimally animate state of existence, by virtue of which it is capable of basking in minute sensory details and of sharing in a "stable state" appreciation for the dynamic equilibrium of all natural forces. Particularly striking, in this regard, is the image of the emerald-headed fly at the conclusion of "An Excursion to the Forest Belt" (*Poezdka v poles'ie*) and the figure of Lukeriya, the visionary "mummy," in "The Live Relic" (*Zhivye Moshchi*). I find persuasive Gershenzon's provocative summation of Turgenev's ultimate vision: "He praised a holism (*tsel'nost'*) wholly without regard to its content from a human perspective." That verdict is uttered in the controversial study of Turgenev's vision and thought, *Mechta i Mysl' Turgeneva*, p. 111.

20.   Sears emphasizes the remarkable placidity with which Henry James accepts a universe whose events are necessarily refracted in pluralistic and unadjudicated human "fictions." (*Negative Imagination*, p. 55.)

21.   Ernest Renan, "Discours prononcé sur la tombe de I. Tourguéneff," included in I. Tourguéneff, *Oeuvres Dernières.* (Paris, 1885).

Bibliography

PRIMARY SOURCES

Writings of Ivan Turgenev

Dimitri Roudine. Hetzel, 1862.
Les Eaux Printanières. Hetzel, 1873.
Lettres de Tourguéneff à Henry James," ed. Jean Seznec. *Comparative Literature* 1 (1949), 193-209.
Manuscrits Parisiens d'Ivan Tourguénev. ed. André Mazon. Champion, 1930.
"Neizdannye Pis'ma I. S. Turgeneva," ed. André Mazon. *Literaturnoe Nasledstvo* 31-32. Moscow, 1937.
Nouvelles Moscovites. Hetzel, 1869.
Oeuvres Dernières. Hetzel, 1885.
Polnoe Sobranie Sochinenii i Pisem. 28 vols. Akademiia Nauk, 1962-1968.
Sobranie Sochinenii v desiati tomakh. 10 vols. Gosizdatkhudlit, 1961-1962.
Turgenev's Letters: A Selection. ed. Edgar H. Lehrman. Knopf, 1961.

Writings of Henry James

A Small Boy & Others. Scribner, 1913.
"Alphonse Daudet," *Century* 26 (1883), 498-509.
Confidence. ed. Herbert Ruhm. Grosset & Dunlap, 1962.
Eight Uncollected Tales. ed. Edna Kenton. Rutgers, 1950.
French Poets and Novelists. ed. Leon Edel. Grosset & Dunlap, 1964.
"Ivan Turgenef's New Novel," *Nation* 24 (1877), 252-53.
"Ivan Turgéniew," *North American Review* 118 (1874), 326-56.
Literary Reviews and Essays. ed. Albert Mordell. Twayne, 1957.
Notes and Reviews. Dunster House, Harvard, 1921.
Notes of a Son and Brother. Scribner, 1914.
Partial Portraits. Macmillan, 1888.
Roderick Hudson. Osgood, 1876.
Selected Letters. ed. Leon Edel. Farrar, Straus, 1955.
The American. Osgood, 1877.
The Art of Fiction and Other Essays. ed. Morris Roberts. Oxford, 1948.
The Art of the Novel: Critical Prefaces. ed. R. P. Blackmur. Scribner, 1934.
The Complete Tales, 12 vols. ed. Leon Edel. Hart-Davis, 1962-1964.
The Future of the Novel: Essays on the Art of Fiction. ed. Leon Edel. Vintage, 1956.
The Letters of Henry James, vol. 1. ed. Percy Lubbock. Scribner, 1920.
The Middle Years. Macmillan, 1917.
The Notebooks. ed. F. O. Matthiessen and Kenneth B. Murdock. Oxford, 1947.
The Novels and Tales. 24 vols. Scribner, 1909.
Views and Reviews. ed. LeRoy Phillips. Ball Publishing, 1908.

SECONDARY MATERIALS

General Works

Auerbach, Erich. *Mimesis: The Representation of Reality in Western Literature*. Doubleday, 1957.
Becker, George J., ed. *Documents of Modern Literary Realism*. Princeton, 1963.
Bennett, E. K. and H. M. Waidson. *A History of the German Novelle*. Cambridge, 1965.

The Clement Vision

Bersani, Leo. *Balzac to Beckett: Center and Circumference in French Fiction.* Oxford, 1970.

Bewley, Marius. *The Complex Fate: Hawthorne, Henry James, and some other American writers.* Chatto & Windus, 1952.

Bourget, Paul. *Nouveaux Essais de Psychologie Contemporaine.* Lemerre, 1886.

Demetz, Peter. "Defenses of Dutch Painting and the Theory of Realism," *Comparative Literature* 15 (1963), 97-115.

DuVal, Thaddeus Ernest, Jr. *The Subject of Realism in the Revue des Deux Mondes, 1831-1865.* University of Pennsylvania, 1936.

Erlich, Victor. *Russian Formalism: History-Doctrine.* Mouton, 1955.

Falk, Robert P. "The Literary Criticism of the Genteel Decades: 1870-1900," *The Development of American Literary Criticism*, ed. Floyd Stovall. North Carolina, 1955.

―――. *The Victorian Mode in American Fiction, 1865-1885.* Michigan State, 1965.

Fanger, Donald. *Dostoevsky and Romantic Realism: A Study of Dostoevsky in Relation to Balzac, Dickens, and Gogol.* Phoenix, 1967.

Freeborn, Richard. *The Rise of the Russian Novel.* Cambridge, 1973.

Friedman, Norman. "Point of View in Fiction: The Development of a Critical Concept," *PMLA* 70 (1955), 1160-84.

Frye, Northrop. *Anatomy of Criticism.* Princeton, 1957.

Grant, Damian. *Realism.* Methuen, 1970.

Haertel, Martin Henry. "German Literature in American Magazines: 1846 to 1880," *Bulletin of University of Wisconsin Philology and Literature Series* 4 (1908).

Hardy, Barbara. *The Appropriate Form: An Essay on the Novel.* Athlone Press, 1964.

Hawthorne, Julian. "Agnosticism in American Fiction," *Princeton Review* 13 (1884), 1-16.

Hemmings, F. W. J. *The Russian Novel in France.* Oxford, 1950.

Howells, W. D. *My Literary Passions.* Harper, 1895.

Iknayan, Marguerite. *The Idea of the Novel in France: The Critical Reaction 1815-1848.* E. Droz, 1961.

Jost, François. "La Tradition du Bildungsroman," *Comparative Literature* 21 (1969), 97-115.

Kolb, Harold H. Jr. *The Illusion of Life: American Realism as a Literary Form.* Virginia, 1969.

Krieger, Murray. *The Tragic Vision; Variations on a Theme in Literary Interpretation.* Chicago, 1960.

Lathrop, G. P. "Growth of the Novel," *Atlantic* 33 (1874), 684-97.

―――. "The Novel and its Future," *Atlantic* 34 (1874), 313-24.

Levin, Harry. *The Gates of Horn: A Study of Five French Realists.* Oxford, 1963.

Lukacs, Georg. *Studies in European Realism.* Grosset & Dunlap, 1964.

Martin, Jay. *Harvests of Change: American Literature, 1865-1914.* Prentice-Hall, 1967.

McMahon, Helen. *Criticism of Fiction: A Study of Trends in the Atlantic Monthly, 1857-1898.* Bookman Associates, 1952.

Merimée, Prosper. *Portraits Historiques et Littéraires.* Lévy, 1874.

Mott, Frank Luther. *A History of American Magazines: 1865-1885.* Harvard, 1938.

Mudrick, Marvin. "Character and Event in Fiction," *Yale Review* 50 (1961), 202-18.

Phelps, Gilbert. *The Russian Novel in English Fiction.* Hutchinson, 1956.

Poggioli, Renato. "Realism in Russia," *Comparative Literature* 3 (1951), 253-67.

Pritchett, V. S. *The Living Novel & Other Appreciations.* Random House, 1964.

Rourke, Constance. *American Humor: A Study of the National Character.* Doubleday, 1953.

Scherer, Edmond. *Etudes sur la Littérature Contemporaine*, vols. 4-5. Lévy, 1874; 1878.

Schmidt, Julian. *Bilder aus dem Geistigen Leben unserer Zeit*, Vol. 1. Grunow, 1870.
Schroder, Maurice Z. "The Novel as a Genre," *Massachusetts Review* (Winter, 1963).
Silz, Walter. *Realism and Reality: Studies in the German Novelle of Poetic Realism*. University of North Carolina Studies in the Germanic Languages and Literatures, 11 (1954).
Tanner, Tony. *The Reign of Wonder: Naivety and Reality in American Literature*. Harper & Row, 1967.
Weinberg, Bernard. *French Realism: The Critical Reaction, 1830-1870*. Chicago, 1937.

Special Studies

Alekseev, M. P., ed. *Turgenevskii Sbornik*, I. "Nauka," 1964.
Anderson, Quentin. *The American Henry James*. Rutgers, 1957.
Batiuto, A. *Turgenev-Romanist*. Izdatelstvo "Nauka," 1972.
Bialy, G. *Turgenev i Ruskii Realizm*. Sovetskii Pisatel', 1962.
Boyesen, Hjalmar H. "A Visit to Tourguéneff," *Galaxy* 17 (1874), 456-66.
Brodianski, Nina. "Turgenev's Short Stories: A Revaluation," *Slavonic and East European Review* 32 (1953), 70-91.
Brodskii, N. L., ed. *I. S. Turgenev: Materialy i Issledovaniia*. Oryol, 1940.
———. *Tvorcheskii Put' Turgeneva*. E. V. Vysotskii, 1923.
Cady, Edwin H. *The Road to Realism*. Syracuse, 1956.
Cambon, Glauco. "The Negative Gesture in Henry James," *Nineteenth Century Fiction* 15 (1961), 335-43.
Cargill, Oscar. "The First International Novel," *PMLA* 53 (1958), 418-25.
———. *The Novels of Henry James*. Macmillan, 1961.
Carter, Everett. *Howells and the Age of Realism*. Lippincott, 1954.
Clark, Sir Kenneth. "Provincialism." Oxford, 1962.
Cortissoz, Royal. *John LaFarge: A Memoir and a Study*. Houghton-Mifflin, 1911.
Davie, Donald. "Turgenev in England: 1850-1950," *Studies in Russian and Polish Literature*, ed. Zbigniew Folejewski. Mouton, 1962, 168-84.
Dupee, F. W. *Henry James*. Sloane, 1951.
Edel, Leon. *Henry James: The Untried Years*. Lippincott, 1953.
———. *Henry James: The Conquest of London, 1870-1881*. Lippincott, 1962.
———. *Henry James: The Middle Years*. Lippincott, 1962.
Fisher, V. M. "Povest' i Roman u Turgeneva," *Tvorchestvo Turgeneva*, ed. I. N. Rozanov and Yu. M. Sokolov. "Zadruga," 1920, 3-39.
Freeborn, Richard. *Turgenev: The Novelist's Novelist, A Study*. Oxford, 1960.
Frierson, William C. and Herbert Edwards. "Impact of French Naturalism on American Critical Opinion, 1877-1892," *PMLA* 63 (1948), 1007-16.
Fryckstedt, Olov W. *In Quest of America: A Study of Howells' Early Development as a Novelist*. Harvard, 1958.
Gabel', M. O. "*Dnevnik Lishnego Cheloveka*: ob avtorskoi otsenke geroia," *Turgenevskii Sbornik*, II. Akademiia Nauk, 1966, 118-26.
Gargano, James W. "Daisy Miller: An Abortive Quest for Innocence," *South Atlantic Quarterly* 59 (1960), 114-20.
Gershenzon, M. *Mechta i Mysl' I. S. Turgeneva*. Brown Slavic Reprint, 1970.
Gettmann, Royal A. *Turgenev in England and America*. Illinois Studies in Language and Literature 27 (1941).
Gippius, Vasilii. "O kompozitsii turgenevskikh romanov," *Venok Turgenevu: Sbornik Statei*. A. A. Ivasenko, 1919, 25-55.
Glasrud, Clarence A. *Hjalmar Hjorth Boyesen*. Norwegian-American Historical Association, 1963.
Granjard, Henri. *Ivan Tourguénev et les courants politiques et sociaux de son temps*. Institut D'Etudes Slaves, 1966.
Grossman, Leonid. *Portret Manon Lesko: Dva Etiuda o Turgeneve*. Moscow, 1922.

The Clement Vision

Haight, Gordon S. "Realism Defined: William Dean Howells," *Literary History of the United States*, ed. Robert E. Spiller. Macmillan, 1948, 878-98.

Halperine-Kaminsky, E. *Tourguéneff and his French Circle*. Holt, 1898.

Hamilton, Eunice C. "Henry James's The Princess Casamassima and Turgenev's Virgin Soil," *SAQ* 61 (1962), 354-64.

Harlow, Virginia. *Thomas Sergeant Perry: A Biography*. Duke, 1950.

Howells, Mildred, ed. *Life in Letters of William Dean Howells*, I. Doubleday, 1928.

Howells, W. D. "Henry James, Jr.," *Century* 25 (1882), 25-29.

James, Henry, ed. *The Letters of Wm. James*, I. Atlantic Monthly Press, 1920.

Kelley, Cornelia Pulsifer. *The Early Development of Henry James*. Illinois Studies in Language and Literature, 1-2 (1930).

Kurliandskaia, G. "Problema kharaktera v romanakh Turgeneva," *Voprosy Literatury* 9 (1958), 64-78.

Leavis, F. R. "Henry James's First Novel," *Scrutiny* 14 (1947), 295-301.

Leavis, Q. D. "Henry James: The Stories," *Scrutiny* 14 (1947), 223-29.

Lebowitz, Naomi. *The Imagination of Loving: Henry James's Legacy to the Novel*. Wayne State, 1965.

Le Clair, Robert C. *Young Henry James, 1843-1870*. Bookman Associates, 1955.

Lerner, Daniel. "The Influence of Turgenev on Henry James," *Slavonic Yearbook* 20 (1941), 28-54.

Mahieu, Robert G. *Sainte-Beuve aux États-Unis*. Princeton, 1945.

Matlaw, Ralph E. *The Composition of Turgenev's Novels*. Unpublished dissertation. Harvard, 1954.

———. "Turgenev's Art in Spring Torrents," *Slavonic and East European Review* 35 (1956), 157-71.

Matthiessen, F. O. *The James Family*. Knopf, 1947.

Pacey, Desmond. "Henry James and his French Contemporaries," *American Literature* 13 (1941), 240-56.

Perry, T. S. "Ivan Turgeneff," *Nation* 12 (1871), 340-41.

———. "Ivan Turgénieff," *Atlantic Monthly* 33 (1874), 565-75.

———. "Julian Schmidt: A German Critic," *Atlantic* 34 (1874), 207-14.

———. "Victor Cherbuliez," *Atlantic* 37 (1876), 279-87.

———. "William Dean Howells," *Century* 23 (1882), 68-85.

Poirier, Richard. *The Comic Sense of Henry James: A Study of the Early Novels*. Oxford, 1967.

Price, Lawrence Marsden. *The Attitude of Gustav Freytag and Julian Schmidt Toward English Literature, 1848-1862*. Johns Hopkins, 1915.

Putt, S. Gorley. *Henry James: A Reader's Guide*. Cornell, 1966.

Roberts, Morris. *Henry James's Criticism*. Harvard, 1929.

Robinson, Edwin Arlington, ed. *Selections from the Letters of Thomas Sergeant Perry*. Macmillan, 1929.

Sears, Sallie. *The Negative Imatination: Form and Perspective in the Novels of Henry James*. Cornell, 1968.

Seyersted, Per E. "Turgenev's Interest in America," *Scando-Slavica* 11 (1965), 25-39.

Snow, Lotus. "The Pattern of Innocence Through Experience in the Characters of Henry James," *University of Toronto Quarterly* 22 (1953), 230-36.

Spender, Stephen. "The School of Experience in the Early Novels," *Hound & Horn* 7 (1934), 417-33.

Tremblay, Napoleon. *La Critique Littéraire d'Edmond Scherer*. Brown University, 1932.

Trilling, Lionel. "The Princess Casamassima," *The Liberal Imagination: Essays on Literature and Society*. Doubleday, 1953.

Tseitlin, A. G. *Masterstvo Turgeneva-Romanista*. Sovetskii Pisatel', 1958.

Vaid, Krishna Baldev. *Technique in the Tales of Henry James*. Harvard, 1964.

Ward, J. A. *The Search for Form: Studies in the Structure of James's Fiction*. North Carolina, 1967.

Wegelin, Christof. *The Image of Europe in Henry James*. Southern Methodist, 1958.

_____ . "The Rise of the International Novel," *PMLA* 77 (1962), 305-10.

Wellek, René. "Henry James's Literary Theory and Criticism," *AL* 30 (1958), 293-321.

Wilson, Edmund. "Turgenev and the Life-Giving Drop," *Ivan Turgenev: Literary Reminiscences and Autobiographical Fragments.* Farrar-Straus, 1958, 3-64.

Woodcock, George. "The Elusive Ideal: Notes on Turgenev," *Sewanee Review* 69 (1961), 34-47.

Yarmolinsky, Avrahm. *Turgenev: The Man, His Art and His Age.* Collier Books, 1961.

Index

Index

DATE DUE

	PRINTED IN U.S.A.